Praise for W

"Traci puts a voice to what so many successful leaders have secretly wondered: What if I stepped off the treadmill? Will I be happier? What is next? Or, to borrow from the Reba hit, Is there life out there? Her thoughtful insights provide a framework to think proactively about transition."

—**SARAH TRAHERN**, CEO, Country Music Association

"If you're thinking about what comes next in your career and your life, you'll benefit from Traci's insights and recommendations in this practical guide for navigating your future and finding more meaning. Traci knows what it's like to have a successful career but to feel that something is missing, because she's been there. For nearly thirty years as a friend and as a colleague at HGTV, I've benefited from Traci's advice and guidance, and now others can too."

—**BURTON JABLIN**, Co-founder of HGTV and former COO of Scripps Networks

"This book is like a mentor in your pocket. But not just any mentor. Traci presents a practical framework for moving forward when you're feeling stuck. It's not full of platitudes and empty advice. Instead, it's packed with helpful tools and ways of thinking that guide you toward setting an actionable vision for a future you actually want. It's about ensuring you're intentional about where you're going, instead of just letting it happen to you. Every leader needs this book."

—**NANCY LYONS**, author of *Work Like a* Boss and CEO of Clockwork

"I loved this book. Traci has tapped into a deep yearning among a lot of 'successful people' to add a sense of significance to their life. The writing offers a humane and practical guide for thinking through what your next life can be and the meaningful things that you can still accomplish. I'm very glad to have this book as a starting point."

—**JOHN DAILEY**, Senior Vice President, Warner Bros. Discovery

"Traci's incredibly hopeful book comes at the perfect time, given how COVID has unraveled our relationships to work. She urges us to ask soul questions: What is this treadmill I'm on? Is there more to my life than work? What does purpose look like for me? Then she gives us processes to find answers. This is a wisdom book for the ages."

—**SUSAN PACKARD**, author of *Fully Human* and *New Rules of the Game*

"After years of knowing what's next, it can be scary when something doesn't feel right anymore, or when we are uncertain what our next move should be. Traci has traveled that path and wrestled with all those questions. With this book, she is now your guide to clarity on who you really are and what you have been uniquely designed to do. This book is a guide to redefining success on your own terms and discovering the life you were meant to live."

—**CHRISTINE OLSON**, Senior Vice President, A+E Networks

"So many of us think, What would I do if I left my job, got laid off, or wanted to chase my true passion? The reality is most people are too scared to do what Traci had the courage to do. Thankfully in this book she shares her formula to tackle our fears and create the strategy for

personal fulfillment and success. Traci's guidance and tutelage enable us to realize our real dreams!"

—**LYNNE LEVEY**, Senior Vice President, Paramount

"It takes bravery to walk away from a successful leadership role and jump into the uncharted. Traci's relatable and authentic experience inspires you to reflect on what you want for yourself and those around you—to help you find what success means for you, and to answer the question, 'Who will I be when this job ends?'"

—**KARLA SANTI**, CEO, Blend Interactive

"Traci masterfully marries her natural wisdom with authentic experience and thoughtful process to create a roadmap for meaningful living. She helps readers discover, embrace, and begin to script the blank pages in life's second act. I highly recommend this book to everyone."

—**NATALIE CONWAY**, Senior Vice President, Publicis Media

"I was impressed by Traci's courage, when at the top of her career, she decided to embark on a new path. Traci embodies the leadership characteristics that have endured the test of time: Honesty, Integrity, Transparency, Vision, Empathy, Communication, Goal Orientation, and most of all a wonderful Heart. She is the perfect person to help others explore the journey to a life of significance, and this book is filled with the wisdom to get you there."

—**STEVE GIGLIOTTI**, Former Chief Revenue Officer,
Scripps Networks Interactive

TRACI SCHUBERT BARRETT

WHAT IF THERE'S MORE?

Finding *Significance* Beyond Success

What If There's More?
Finding Significance beyond Success

For permission requests, speaking inquires, and bulk order purchase options please contact info@navigatethejourney.com.

For additional resources and to reach out to author directly, go to www.tracischubertbarrett.com

Published by Lioncrest Publishing
Austin, TX
www.lioncrest.com

Library of Congress Cataloging-in-Publication Data

Library of Congress Control Number: 2022914868

ISBN 978-1-5445-2824-3 Hardcover
978-1-5445-2823-6 Paperback
978-1-5445-2822-9 Ebook

This book is presented solely for educational and informational purposes. The author and publisher are not offering professional advice. This book contains advice and information relating to health care. It should be used to supplement rather than replace the advice of your doctor or another trained professional. It is recommended that you seek your physician's advice before embarking on any medical program or treatment.

Some names and identifying details have been changed to protect the privacy of the individuals.

Printed in the United States of America

Cover design by Teresa Muniz.

This book is for my beautiful daughters,

Bronagh and Ashling.

You are fearfully and wonderfully made.

Be You.

This book is because of my amazing husband, Tom.

Thank you for believing in me.

If you don't like the road you're walking,
start paving another one.

—DOLLY PARTON

CONTENTS

PART TWO

WHY DO I EXIST?

PART THREE

WHERE AM I GOING?

INTRODUCTION

I'm sitting in my corner office in a fabulous building in downtown Chicago overlooking Lake Michigan and beautiful Millennium Park. I feel like I'm literally and figuratively at the top of the world. I'm running two offices for one of the most successful and beloved television networks, which I helped launch nearly two decades earlier. I'm more financially successful than I had ever imagined, and I love the people I work with and for. It's been a wild ride, and I have made it.

I should be excited. I'm waiting to leave the office to attend another marvelous event. We've rented out the Chicago Theater, and I'm preparing to entertain clients, along with famed talent like the Property Brothers, who, yes, are just as lovely in person. I'm going to eat well and drink great wine.

So why do I feel off? Unsatisfied, restless?

There's not much I don't like about my job. Yes, it's stressful. The media industry is no picnic, but I'm well liked here, feel safe, laugh with my colleagues, admire my mentors, and have great pride in the network I represent. But there has been a shift. I'm rather certain it came right after my fortieth birthday when I began to notice even though I've come a long way, I couldn't stop wondering if there's more.

I've pretty much grown up at HGTV. I took this job at age twenty-four. It was risky taking a job for a television network that didn't yet exist, had no programming, and was without a current office space. We had no human resources department and only a handful of people. At that age, I felt like I didn't have much to lose and if the whole thing was a bust, I'd at least have some entrepreneurial startup experience on my resume. I was ready for an adventure, and that is precisely what I got.

It took a few years, but eventually, we moved from gingham and gardening to *House Hunters* and *Flip or Flop*. I rose up the ranks very quickly, especially by media conglomerate standards. We started another network called DIY, bought the Food Network, started the Cooking Channel, and eventually became Scripps Networks. In what seemed like the blink of an eye, we were a bona fide media company. I no longer had to spend ten minutes explaining what HGTV was and how you could watch it in certain cities. Now it was everywhere, and everyone was watching. I felt proud, accomplished, well known, and envied. I had reached a level of success I had never imagined.

While my career was soaring, some other things in my life were calling. I had two young daughters with a great husband, who also had a very demanding job. We were stretched thin. I longed to be with my daughters but found myself on a plane to HGTV's two headquarters in New York or Knoxville more often than I liked.

Being in management had its perks, but it also came with enormous responsibilities and demands. Each time the plane took off, I thought how unnatural it felt to be in the air so often when my children were on the ground. I was also deeply involved in our church and doing some serious soul searching about the purpose of it all. Was I just going through the motions? Was I more focused on success and making others happy? Was there deeper meaning to be found?

I was always an overachiever, passing one mile marker after another. High school honor student, check. College graduate, check. Married with children, check. Flashy job with a big paycheck, check. New house, check. I was happy, but a bit overwhelmed from the never-ending treadmill of success.

The life I had built with my husband, along with the pressures of my job, had become too much to handle. The media kept telling me that women could have it all. *But could we?* If I had it all, why was I crying when the plane took off? Why did I find going to another fabulous Dream Home Giveaway trip an inconvenience? Drinking wine in Sonoma, California, with famous HGTV talent was a hassle? *What was happening?* I wasn't unhappy, but I wasn't at peace.

I needed a significant reset.

I found myself at a crossroads. I was wrestling with so many questions that arise at midlife. For two years, the questions that ran through my head were constant. *Is this all there is? Can I find true meaning in my work? What do I really want? Am I allowed to ask what I want?*

What if there's more?

Rather than searching for those answers amid my day-to-day grind, and much to the bewilderment of my bosses, I quit. It was awfully hard, and there were many tears. I grieved the loss of a long, proud, and familiar path, but I simply had to make a change. When I woke up the next morning, I felt a deep sense of relief. I had absolutely no idea what to do next, or if staying home with my girls would be enough for me. I never thought my journey would bring me here, but I had just pulled the trigger and now sat on the other side of my fabulous career.

THE NEW CROSSROADS

Throughout my career at HGTV and beyond, I have encountered hundreds of business leaders who have found themselves on the same treadmill I was on. While experiences, income levels, and locations vary, the fervent need to catch a mid-career breath and gain perspective becomes almost universal.

If you picked up this book, perhaps you too, have reached the pinnacle of your success, working your entire life to build everything you now have. However, instead of feeling fulfilled and content, you find yourself more resigned and strained. The worst part is you don't know why, and no one around you understands your dissatisfaction.

If these new crossroads could talk, they'd ask you these key questions: How did I get here? Why do I exist? Where am I going?

If you don't have clear answers to these questions, you'll likely wind up in the dreaded midlife crisis. The feeling of being stuck with no answers can lead to depression or a desire to escape. This desire can sometimes get lived out through counterproductive choices, like having an affair, hastily filing for divorce, or buying a red sports car.

The sad news is that these choices rarely bring the answers you are seeking. However, there is a way to lean into these questions and not only find the answers but use the answers to develop a map for the future ahead. Which brings us to the good news: the second half of your life can actually be brighter and more meaningful than your first.

THE LONG ROAD AHEAD

It may be surprising to discover that this maturing season of life is still full of so many incessant questions. But keep in mind being able to have a full life after midlife is pretty unprecedented, making our future more uncertain than we once expected it to be. Half the babies born in the West in 2007 are predicted to live to 104 years old.[1] Half! A century ago, there was only a 1 percent chance of living to that age.

When life was shorter and more predictable, there wasn't much planning needed. In past generations, far less thought was given to one's life journey and choices because there weren't nearly as many options. As a result, our grandparents saw life as short and fragile, and due to experiences like the stock market crash of 1929 and the Great Depression, they were happy to settle for the comfort of predictability and a good living.

Not only are our generation and the ones behind us living longer, but most of us are also living *healthier* longer, giving us more time and ability to work and engage with society. The age of technology has opened doors that were previously unimaginable. The choices before us are endless, but so, too, is the uncertainty, it seems.

It can be scary when thinking about how to finance a longer life or how to stay healthy, but there is also a newfound luxury of considering two or three different careers. We can choose to see these modern opportunities as a gift, especially if we think through our options and plan properly for this new future. Seeing possible paths is a great motivator to forge a new one. As we progress through this longer life, it's good and even essential to learn how to become more innovative and flexible to change in order to stretch our perspectives in ways we never have before.

Ultimately, these new crossroads are an invitation to regain a sense of agency over your years to come. In the chapters that follow you will learn how to navigate your own journey and make the intentional decisions necessary to truly thrive.

Life can remain a long slog on the treadmill or become a bigger adventure full of *significance*—welcome to the new crossroads.

ANOTHER BLANK PAGE

Bruce Springsteen had a one-man concert residency on Broadway aptly titled *Springsteen on Broadway.*

In a prelude to his song "Thunder Road," he spoke of his youth and leaving home:

Maybe there's nothing like that moment in your life of being young and leaving someplace, all that youthful freedom. You feel finally being untethered from everything you've ever known. The life you've lived, your past, your parents, the world you've gotten used to and that you've loved and hated. Your life lying before you like a blank page. It's the one thing I miss about getting older, I miss the beauty of that blank page. So much life in front of you. Its promise, its possibilities, its mysteries, its adventures. That blank page just lying there. Daring you to write on it.

I remember so well that same feeling of a blank page when I permanently left home right after graduating from college. I had $500 cash from graduation gifts, about $25,000 of college debt, and no job. I had a head full of dreams but no clear plan.

I remember my dad hugging me goodbye as I stood on the corner of Sedgwick and Webster in downtown Chicago. His final words to me were "Get a job."

This was a blank page that almost everyone I had graduated with was also facing. Post-college resumes had been carefully crafted, and the world was our oyster. We were collectively hitting the pavement, bright-eyed and bushy-tailed. The page dared us to write on it, and we were happy to pick up the pen.

But there was another time in my life when that same blank page before me caused feelings that were much more mixed. I remember walking downstairs the morning after my going-away party from HGTV and looking out the back windows of my house. For the first time since I was twenty-one years old, I had no job and no clear plans for the next phase of life. Blank page.

Yet this time it was different. I had made an unorthodox decision at the height of my success to change course. I made a leap from

HGTV without the support of a rule book, manual, societal guidelines, or even the company of others on the journey.

Instead of feeling like the world was my oyster, I felt naked. Stripped of my work identity, proximity to the social network I had enjoyed, and the platform on which I displayed my talents and gifts, I was forced to reckon with who I truly was and what I truly wanted. With more years behind me, I knew I also had more wisdom. However, I was surprised to realize that I now also had more fear. It was the kind of fear that would do everything in its power to hold me back from embracing the possibility of the blank page that lay before me.

While The Boss, at age seventy-one, lamented the loss of blank pages from the past, I wrote this book to help you rediscover, and even rejoice, that blank pages don't just belong to our youth anymore. There is more.

CROSSROADS QUESTIONS

Shortly after I left HGTV, I went through a process of answering those big key questions for myself. It was the first time in my life when I had taken a serious pause and systematically looked at all areas of my life, even those outside of work. I thought about what the future might look like if I decided to live out my purpose and passions. I defined my unique talents and envisioned how I might live them out in all areas of my life. I intentionally articulated a vision and created a roadmap for my future. The process pulled me out of my "stuck-ness" and pointed me in the right direction.

From there I built a new business that aligned with my dreams. I merged my decades of corporate business and executive leadership experience with my psychology training, and started Navigate the Journey, a business consulting firm. Alongside my husband, we use proven processes in strategic planning and team building to help entrepreneurs and business executives achieve success. We have coached many CEO and C-suite executives to a deeper understanding of who they are and how they are wired.

As a result of this new strategic way of looking at my life, I am currently and continually focused on living out a life of significance. Today I feel like the captain of my own ship. With a clearer understanding of my unique purpose, I have built the life I want and have found a new and more sustainable contentment.

By society's standards, being a top HGTV executive is the pinnacle of success, but what I couldn't put my finger on until years later was how I was longing for more clarity around my significance.

Rather than being defined by what you do, by answering key questions and looking at your life with a strategic lens, you can discover who you are and then how to live that out through all areas of your life. Therefore, no matter your path, role, or station in life, you can find fulfillment.

The process of answering these key crossroads questions is designed to take you to a deeper place, a place of intention. It provides you with not only purpose but a roadmap to your ultimate life's vision.

My process for creating what I call a Strategic Life Map™ is a culmination of years of coaching, strategic planning, psychological assessment debriefs, and exit planning. I have been influenced by what I believe to be the best of various philosophies out there along with my own successful techniques to create a framework that is simple yet extremely powerful. It is from my own experience and that of my clients that I'd like to share with you the power of implementing this framework for yourself.

COME ON A JOURNEY

This book is your invitation to go on a journey toward a new way of looking at yourself, your life, and the immediate world around you. It is an invitation to discover more. More of who you are and the significant impact you can have. There is no end to the journey of discovery, *sans* death. The goal is not to know it all, achieve it all, or even to be fully known by the world. Instead, this is a journey of growth and discovery. A journey of impact and purpose. A journey to enjoy and lean into rather than a race to the finish line.

Part of the excitement and joy of life is learning, growing, and developing into a better version of yourself each and every day.

> ***When I let go of the idea of my perfect self and replace it with my purposeful self, I feel great joy, which enables me to create goals to advance something larger than myself.***

When I let go of my ego, which guides me to achieve for my own glory and gain, I am more willing and able to give my time and resources to the betterment of those around me. Sacrifice for perfection or pride drains, saps, depresses, and depletes. Sacrifice for purpose fulfills, completes, enables, and energizes. Perfection and pride may give you short-term wins, and those wins may feel great in the moment, yet they are fleeting. Purpose is the long game. Purpose is the quest for a true and lasting legacy.

The more famous or well-known people you revere in this world are no better than you. They are human. They have the same raw materials as you; they've just tapped into them. They know who they are and what they want to do. They have clarity. Take it from Steve Jobs, who once said, "Everything around you that you call life was made up by people that were no smarter than you. And you can change it, you can influence it…once you learn that, you'll never be the same again."

This book is designed to provide you with a framework toward a new vision of yourself and your future. This book is for those who are open to embracing the possibility of a longer life, who wish to push through cynicism and grab hold of a new perspective on who they are, where they've been, and where they are headed to ultimately understand how they can best impact the world around them for good. This book is for people who are excited for the long life ahead and for those who yearn to leave a legacy behind for those future centenarians rising up after them.

It is time to give up your comfort and shake off your expectations, as well as the expectations of others in your life. If you are ready to drop any cynicism and pessimism and take ownership of *you,* I invite you to continue reading.

Let's create a map to discover more. A map to the future you've always wanted—or that you're just discovering you might want—one that matters to you and those around you. A life *of significance.*

HOW TO USE THIS BOOK

As the following chapters will guide you to understand, the road to significance is often marked by answering key questions that arise at the major crossroads of life:

How Did I Get Here?
Why Do I Exist?
Where Am I Going?

I have divided this book into three parts to reflect this journey. As you answer these questions, you will discover a framework for reflecting on your past, discerning the realities of your present, and designing a life you want for the future.

Part One: How Did I Get Here?

We all have a story, but we don't often, if ever, look at the whole picture. Looking back and understanding your past, the patterns and beliefs that you have developed thus far, is essential to understanding how you got to where you are today and identifying what you want to be different tomorrow. To move toward the life you want, you must work to rectify your limiting patterns or beliefs and adopt a new and proper mindset for the future chapters of your great story.

Part Two: Why Do I Exist?

A compass is one of the most important instruments for navigation. Your Life Compass is an essential tool we will build together that is composed of your talents, passions, values, and purpose. A life of significance recognizes that you are more than just your profession. When you are able to see your Life Zones, or key life priorities, from a 360-degree angle, you are able to optimize each day and live with greater purpose. We will examine your Life Zones in three buckets: your personal health, your village, and your work.

Part Three: Where Am I Going?

Crafting a vivid picture of your most desired future is a powerful process that transforms your psyche from one focused on success to one of significance. You will design a Legacy Statement articulating how you want to be remembered and create a new lens through which to see your future. You will also outline goals and learn the tools necessary to execute and realize the life you want.

REMINDERS FOR YOUR ROAD AHEAD

My best advice to you as you go through the process of reading this book is to take a deep breath and know that this is a journey of progression, not a race to perfection.

This is often easier said than done, which is why I've placed "Reflections" at the close of each chapter. This book is not about just hearing from me, but it is also about hearing from you. The truth lies within you, and this book is the roadmap to unlocking the answer to that burning question: *What If There's More?*

Most of us will live relatively ordinary lives and die ordinary deaths, but that doesn't mean we can't leave behind a positive legacy. I want my life to be not just a history of me but the *history of the mission of me*. If you want the same, then push through the hard questions and keep reading to the end. The common pursuit of success is a road many have traveled. The pursuit of significance is one far less traveled. Join me on this new road. Trust me; there is more, and your very best chapters are yet to come.

PART ONE

HOW DID I GET HERE?

Sometimes you have to grow up before you appreciate how you grew up.

—DANIEL BLACK

CHAPTER ONE

YOUR SUCCESS

"People today have two lives: Life I and Life II. We are over-prepared for Life I, and we are under-prepared for Life II. There is no university for the second half of life."

—PETER DRUCKER

I had developed a fear of flying. This seemed very odd to me as I was typically the person falling asleep during takeoff. I loved traveling and thought of it as a perk to my job. Now my hands gripped the seat tightly. If there was a bump or sound, I was suddenly best friends with the person sitting next to me, gently asking them if they had heard that or felt that. I had become that crazy lady sitting next to you on the plane.

I attributed this newfound phobia to the addition of my husband and kids. Maybe I was scared of flying because I had so much more to lose.

I met with a much-admired professor I had in graduate school while completing my master's of psychology. I told her about my fear of flying, and after a moment of reflection, she said simply, "Sounds like you don't want to die in this job."

"What do you mean?" I asked.

"It seems you have more to do but you just don't know what. You don't want to die before you figure it out."

This hit me so hard that it brought tears to my eyes . . . the power of good therapy. I had so thoroughly planned and executed my career up to that point, but I didn't have anything mapped out for the next stage of my life. I had become vocationally rudderless. It had not occurred to me that all of my success wasn't fulfilling. I was harboring a deeper desire for something else, something more, something greater.

When I shared this new awareness with friends, I found I wasn't alone. This yearning wasn't exclusive to those in corporate America or even to those in the workforce. Many of my stay-at-home mom friends were aching for more clarity.

It wasn't exclusive to men or women. It wasn't exclusive to the highly paid or those solidly in the middle class.

There did seem to be a couple of correlations. The people who felt the same had believed themselves closer to a midlife crossroads. They felt like the formative, climbing-the-corporate-ladder years were behind them. They had experienced a bit of an awakening. They had accomplished all they had hoped or that was expected of them but were completely uncertain about what should come next. And even if they had an idea of what they could do, they certainly didn't have the confidence to make a change. They were firmly planted in their life as it was, but the whispers of their heart were getting louder, asking, "What If There's More?"

LIFE I: THE LIFE YOU HAVE

Often overwhelmed and overcommitted, we can lock ourselves into certain situations believing we don't have a choice. Why is that?

As young children, we didn't typically choose our food, clothes, or even activities—they were all chosen for us.

As we moved into tween and teenage years, we started to individualize and embrace the power of choice. We were given some space to choose a sport or join a club. We chose friends, or often they chose us.

Next we moved into the momentous choice of college, although there were typically boundaries dictated by our high school performance or our parents' financial situation.

And then came young adulthood, where we began to differentiate ourselves from those who raised us and the people we grew up with. We began to experience more fearlessness, optimism, and empowerment. The world was our oyster—even if it was a predetermined oyster leading us directly toward the corporate dream, marriage, or both.

And that brings us to where we are today—many of us climbing the corporate ladder, building that company, and trying to leave legacies for those we love.

Success, right?

But what if along the way we surrendered a bit too much of our courageousness? Maybe we had enough risk-taking audacity for one or two adventures, but now that middle age has approached, all sorts of excuses, fears, and reservations have suddenly taken hold.

When we exchange optimistic hopes for realistic responsibilities, we can become driven by duty alone. Feeling responsible is a necessary, adult thing, but shouldn't we be driven by something more?

Who Do You Want To Be?

Ever since a young age, the adults around us asked, "What do you want to be when you grow up?" Rarely, if ever, were we asked, "Who do you want to be?"

As a result, many of us grew up believing our identity would ultimately be defined by whatever job we took. So we claimed that identity and imagined ourselves within it. It may have even become our first Halloween costume.

This future-focused identity was one of the first goals we set in life. It was the first measure of success—a vision of a goal that, if obtained, would mean "we've made it."

While deep down we know it's who we are as human beings that matters most, this "knowing" often bucks up against the long-standing societal systems that teach us career success is where you will really shine and be noticed. In other words, our outward success becomes more important than our inward success.

But this emphasis on a particular kind of success sets us up for a long-term "What's next?" versus a "Why next?" outlook. Once we've succeeded outwardly, we wake up confused as to why we feel a little stuck or unsatisfied inside. The tools we have amassed to get to the next mile marker aren't working as well at helping us untangle what we want next. Meanwhile, the deepest and truest parts of us lay dormant.

Suddenly one year has been eclipsed by the next, and all along we keep busy by running... in place to nowhere in particular. What's more, the systems we've rooted ourselves in remain stingy on offering us the time, the space, or the grace to reflect, consider, and choose the true direction we want our lives to go in. So we keep running.

It isn't until we notice that more of our life is ending up behind us than ahead that we begin to honestly reflect. As we get a closer view of death or start to see our own loved ones die, we begin to fear, rethink, and doubt what the future may hold.

The Paradox of Success

So many of my clients feel they *should* be happy. They tell me they are extremely fortunate and have nothing legitimate to complain about compared to so many others in the world.

But their dissatisfaction leads to overwhelming feelings of guilt and confusion. It is often only in the safety of a coaching session that the CEO, entrepreneur, working parent, business leader, or PhD will let themselves say the words out loud: "I'm not fulfilled—even though by society's standards I should be."

This state of unfulfillment is more prevalent than most know. Even more confusing, though, is trying to wrap your head around why it exists.

In 2015, *Business Insider* magazine published an article about Markus Persson, the wildly controversial creator of the successful video game Minecraft. Persson became one of the richest, most successful entrepreneurs of our time when he sold his company for a whopping $2.5 billion. After the sale he began living the high life, buying a $70 million mansion, throwing lavish parties often attended by celebrities, and going on high-end vacations.

Amid all this success, when he appeared to be on top of the world, Persson shared the following on Twitter: "The problem with getting everything is you run out of reasons to keep trying. Hanging out with a bunch of friends and partying with famous people, able to do whatever I want, and I have never felt more isolated."[2]

What a twist of fate. You are one of the wealthiest people in the world, but you are feeling a kind of personal poverty that has drained your emotional and relational capital.

Regardless of past achievements, many of us wake up at some point to realize we feel stuck, unfulfilled, or maybe just restless. These feelings are important to notice because they are actually an invitation to unlock pressing questions in our head: *What does it all mean? What do I really want?*

Many are deciding if they can and want to stay where they are and make a bigger impact. *Should I go for that promotion? Should I ask for more, show up better? Should I try to grow my team?*

Others are wrestling with making a change like starting another company, shifting to a rival company, or making a complete career shift and finally following that nagging dream. *Is the grass really greener on the other side? Am I qualified to make a move? Will people think I'm crazy?*

Some people wake up one day and aren't sure what they should do or even who they are. It's as if they are in a new play and haven't yet been given a role. Because life to this point was a list of predetermined mile markers, they are mystified by the lack of clarity on next steps. *Who am I supposed to be now?*

Some have raised children and are on the verge of becoming empty nesters; others have just sold their company, while others have reached the top of the corporate ladder. They all aren't sure what's next, but there is hope for more.

I've done the expected; now what?

Filling the Void

Author, essayist, and Columbia University professor Andrew Delbanco has written extensively on American history and culture. According to Delbanco, "The most striking feature of contemporary culture is the unslaked craving for transcendence."[3]

When we aren't living the life we want, we become hungry. This wanting of transcendence—or desire to go beyond the limits of our ordinary experience—is understood by many scholars to be a natural and basic human need. And one we need to lean into.

In his groundbreaking paper from 1943, *A Theory of Human Motivation*, humanist and psychologist Abraham Maslow wrote that healthy human beings have basic, innate needs.[4] He arranged them in a hierarchy, with the more primitive physiological and safety needs at the bottom of a pyramid and the more dynamic, psychological, and self-fulfillment needs at the top.

Maslow believed the higher needs only come into focus once the lower, more basic needs have been met. He called the bottom needs "deficiency needs" because we do not feel anything if they are met, but if they are not, we can become anxious or stressed out.

Maslow called the top of the pyramid the "growth needs," as they go beyond our present self and drive us to our fullest potential as humans. Self-actualization according to Maslow encompasses morality, creativity, unity, acceptance, purpose, meaning, and inner potential.

From this perspective, the anxiety that many of us feel once we have reached a certain level of success and fulfilled the bottom of the pyramid is our drive for self-actualization. But rather than embracing the bigger picture and pushing into those questions, many of us keep feeding our anxieties by padding up the bottom of the pyramid. We try to acquire more money, more homes, more clothing, and more security. We fill our lives with more friends, more social activities, more degrees, and more recognition.

This "more is more" approach to filling the void ultimately leaves us empty. Without knowing how to embrace a phase of self-awareness and discovery, we end up leading a life that is artificial and inauthentic. We deny our aging, look toward comfort, and reject any invitation to wrestle with the bigger questions of life.

We try to reject that we are steadily unfulfilled and instead take another vacation or work more hours in hopes that the promotion or the new client will bring us peace and satisfaction. Or maybe we just work harder to make our children more successful and hope their victories will reflect well on us, and their success will bring us the fulfillment we crave.

Unfortunately, these attempts, even if successful, are fleeting and, for those with parenting responsibilities, often leave behind more collateral damage than we could ever anticipate: more hours away from home and depressed children who feel like they can never live up to our expectations and have no idea how to advocate for themselves, let alone how to take a loss or manage a failure. It is a path that rarely leads to a happy ending.

What is the way to a happy ending?

Maslow believed that only a small percentage of the human race will self-actualize, because you need to have unique qualities such as self-awareness and emotional maturity to get there.

But I don't think that self-actualization rests with only a few. The real ingredient needed to reach the peak of the pyramid is courage. It's waking up and facing the anxiety of the unknown. It's seeing the big picture of your life and ultimately the realization that this life is finite.

You came into being, and you will one day exit the stage. We are all just passing through. This realization means deciding what your passing through means—what it means to you, what it means to those in your life, and what it means to the world around you.

> ***The answers to life's big questions don't elude us because we are dumb; they elude us because we are numb.***

We are going through the motions, thriving in our busyness, and disconnected from ourselves. We consciously or subconsciously avoid going deep to wrestle with these questions because the answers can bring a call to action and responsibility.

But the reward of going deep is too great to sleep on. The reward is the key to unlocking a life you actually want. A life full of freedom, agency, strength, and impact. It's time to unlock your significance.

LIFE II: THE LIFE YOU WANT

One of the greatest filmmakers of all time, Orson Welles, once said, "If you want a happy ending, that depends on, of course, where you stop your story."

Midlife is not the end of happiness, nor a call for crisis, but rather an invitation to take a deep breath and believe that the second half of your life *can* and *should be* more fulfilling and invigorating than the first half.

Aging Intentionally

I recently came across a photograph of my late grandmother. As I examined the date it was taken and did the math, I was surprised to discover she was only a little bit older than I am right now.

I sat looking at that picture for a long time wondering if she looked further along in her years because those were the days when longevity had a limited life span. Simply put, your "golden years" set in much sooner than they do today.

My grandmother had a lot of class, dressed well, and was sharp as a tack up until her death at age ninety-four. At the time that photo was taken, I doubt she believed she was going to live that long, though I am positive she was resigned to accepting any choices or opportunities ahead of her were limited.

Our parents' and grandparents' generations were conditioned to look at their lives in three key stages: growing up and becoming educated, working adulthood, and retirement. And like one big group project, typically, everyone made transitions from stage to stage at the same point in their lives.

Today, those stages feel more like archaic suggestions. No longer are we working in the same jobs until retirement at age sixty-two. Rather than considering the end of one successful career as the beginning of retirement, many are open to exploring new jobs or even new fields of work. A 2018 Pew Trust survey found that nearly two-thirds of workers polled don't expect to retire at sixty-five, and many surveyed said they never plan to retire. America's average retirement age has increased in the past twenty-five years to sixty-six or older.[5] It seems people have lost track of a set retirement age, with more openly considering extending their working years if they can find greater pleasure, agency, and fulfillment in the work they are doing.

In the book *The New Long Life*, London Business School professors Andrew Scott and Lynda Gratton examine what it means to change your view of age given today's new longevity.

> It is fascinating to realize that only a quarter of how you age is genetically determined. That leaves considerable scope for your own actions, as well as events beyond your control, to exert influence.

Scott and Gratton go on to write, "whatever your age, you have a longer time horizon ahead of you than past generations. This puts a premium on being forward-looking... a longer life and more transitions open up a wider set of possible selves."

When I consider that my grandmother lived during the years of World War I, the Spanish Flu, the Great Depression, and WWII, I can understand why gratitude, security, and comfort were good and right goals in her later life.

The call for my generation and those coming up behind feels quite a bit broader. Our generations have benefited from a more comfortable and less volatile existence. Furthermore, many of us were able to experience an unprecedented pause due to the coronavirus pandemic. This global interruption led many of us to reflect, wonder, and awaken those more profound parts of our soul beyond the predictable and predetermined.

We now have permission and a remarkable opportunity to move beyond "just keeping the lights on" at work or following steps that were already laid and make our next twenty to thirty years matter in a way that's unique to each of us.

I commonly hear my clients say they don't want to wake up one day and realize they just went through the motions, grew stale, or weren't living a purposeful life. My advice is if you want a different story to tell, it's essential to make space and start asking yourself, "What do the next decades hold, and how can I be intentional about defining that?"

Significance Is Calling

The road to significance takes thought, time, and proper perspective. It takes pushing past cynicism and even fear of death to get to a place of clarity around the desire to create a new roadmap for life. This choice is yours and yours alone.

Peter Drucker, hailed as the father of modern management, was the author of thirty-nine books, two-thirds of which he wrote after the age of sixty-five. He gave his last lecture not long before he died at the age of ninety-five. Drucker believed the best years of somebody's life were between the ages of sixty and ninety—and look how that played out for him. Operating from a "best is yet to come" mentality can give you that extra "oomph" to better show up for your team, your company, your kids, and more. You just need a vision for it.

Whatever success you have achieved to this point is a reason to feel proud and even celebrate. If you are reading this book, you have most likely worked very hard to get to where you are and have what you have today. But trust me—the longing for more has a purpose.

President John F. Kennedy once famously said, "Ask not what your country can do for you—ask what you can do for your country."

When it comes to this one life we have, I believe that we should be asking ourselves more than "what do we want from life?", but also "what does life want from us?"

In other words, don't get it twisted. This book isn't an invitation to more self-centered gratification. That way of living only serves as an illusion to a life you *think* you want. But if you want a life of significance, one that will truly fulfill you, you're in for a battle against the unconscious self. It is a leap out of self-centeredness and into self-awareness.

Self-awareness illuminates who you are and guides you to who you want to be.

A life driven only by success is never satisfied because there is always more to achieve and prove. It's time to quiet the drive for success and ignite another drive instead. It's time to embrace purer ambitions that challenge us to turn our talents into purpose and our careers into callings.

CHOOSING LIFE

It's often easy to dream of the life we want but dealing with the obstacles standing in the way is another beast that we are conditioned to avoid. If we want to create a life that excites us, we must remember the status quo will never work to disrupt itself without a plan to both identify obstacles and overcome them.

This is illustrated in the story of North Korean refugee Jessie Kim, who escaped one of the most repressive countries in the world by running across a frozen river to China. Kim's status quo life in North

Korea was stringent and hard, especially following her mother's death. At only eleven years old, Kim survived by peddling food and other goods on the black market. Selling between her grandmother's rural village and nearby Hyesan, and later to China, gave her a taste of the outside world. Once the door cracked open, she was able to see a life that she wanted and decided to escape.

Kim's contacts in China helped her hide, and eventually she made her way to Seoul, where she now lives. Today, she is unveiling some of the North Korean culture to the outside world as a chef who has built her career cooking food that is indigenous to her roots. Kim escaped a life she was given for a life she wanted, all while continuing to keep the thread to her homeland through her cooking.

When retelling her story, Kim profoundly said, "You can't choose your parents. You can't choose your hometown or your country. But you can choose life."

While most of us are not examining our lives within the confines of a Communist country, we often feel confined to life as we know it with no clear way out. As Kim's story so courageously illuminates, the path to building the life you want, a life of significance, begins with choosing life.

The fact that you are holding this book in your hands suggests you have a growing awareness that you are much more than your successes. In the following chapters we will identify obstacles keeping you from the life you want and build a map to not only claim your destination but enjoy the journey along the way.

Reflections

- Reflect on all your achievements to this point.
- How have you defined success?
- What voids do you feel you spend time trying to fill?
- What are you currently craving in your life?

CHAPTER TWO

YOUR SIGNIFICANCE

"We have to get used to the idea
that at the most important crossroads
in life there are no signs."

—ERNEST HEMINGWAY

While joining a startup endeavor has many risks, one of the great opportunities is to rise up in the ranks rather quickly. I worked especially hard in those first years at HGTV and was led by some of the most talented and encouraging bosses and mentors. Their belief and investment in me is something for which I will be forever grateful.

I was promoted to management and ran the Chicago office at the ripe old age of twenty-nine. I remember being outwardly excited but inwardly terrified. At the time, all my counterparts at rival television networks were significantly older and more experienced.

I remember sitting at a dinner with the man who ran the entire sales department for HGTV. He always seemed interested in my success and was often quick to give a kind word of encouragement. I felt safe enough to confess my inner fears of inadequacy to him and then quickly responded to my own doubts with a perky, "I guess you are just supposed to fake it until you make it!"

He turned to me and said, "Well, that doesn't sound like a very authentic route to go."

I replied with a blank stare, as clever responses were escaping me.

He continued, "Great leaders are made, not born. Yes, you have a ways to go, but the road is long for all of us. You'll get there, but always stay true to yourself."

I held on to that advice and settled in for the journey of leadership. He was right. Great leaders are made. While some people are born with innate gifts and talents that may set them up to be a good leader, it is the ones who humbly dedicate themselves to learning and growing, all while staying true to themselves, who are set apart from the pack.

THE QUEST TO BE SOMEBODY

I believe that people who live lives of significance are also made, not born. They don't work to appear smarter, better, or more of an authority than others. They are the courageous ones who shine a light of humility that comes only from someone who gave their ego a rest long enough to search for something more.

I remember the week that Mother Teresa and Princess Diana died. They were the two most recognizable women in the world at the time of their deaths in 1997. They were mirror images of what the world wanted people to be like but with such completely different paths to notoriety.

Almost everyone would love a royal life of fame like Diana, but only one person can marry the Prince of Wales. When you add in the other needed ingredients at the time—blue blood, beautiful, and a virgin—your chances for that marriage proposal are minuscule.

But anyone could be like Mother Teresa. Anyone could dedicate themselves to a life of good in the world and positive impact. Anyone can dedicate themselves to a life of significance.

Sadly, many of us prefer the glory and fame of celebrity, even if meaningless, as opposed to an impact like Mother Teresa, which comes through a life of sacrifice and humility.

Why, for some of us, isn't it enough to live a quiet, ordinary life with an extraordinary impact?

Oftentimes we can mistake significance for glory and fame. When we get a taste of it, not only do we want more, but the fear of losing it becomes real. The fear of being ordinary or mediocre can set in. In short, it feels good, and we can get addicted to that feeling.

Even the biggest celebrities of our time have difficulty grappling with their self-worth in the quest for continued notoriety.

Madonna, the Queen of Pop, the top-selling female artist of all time, has achieved glory and fame in a career that has spanned four decades. In a *Vanity Fair* interview at the height of her career, Madonna said,

> My drive in life comes from a fear of being mediocre. That is always pushing me. I push past one spell of it and discover myself as a special human being but then I feel I am still mediocre and uninteresting unless I do something else. Because even though I have become somebody, I still have to prove that I AM somebody.[6]

While some people may find this quote shocking, I find it refreshingly honest. Madonna was at the top of her game when she gave this interview. A famous, global superstar. A material girl living in her fabulous material world. Yet here is one of the most recognizable humans on the face of the earth, confessing a fear that many overachievers never say aloud. Mediocracy can feel like death.

In the timeless bestselling book *The 7 Habits of Highly Effective People*, Stephen Covey examines this phenomenon. He discovered that high achievers are often plagued with a sense of emptiness.

Covey outlines in the beginning of his book two different kinds of success. Before World War I, success was measured by what he called "Character Ethic." Characteristics such as humility, fidelity, integrity, courage, and justice were attributed to a person's success. Post WWI, things shifted. Success became attributed to what he refers to as "Personality Ethic." Society now measures success as a function of personality, public image, behaviors, and skills.

Covey notices that Personality Ethic is shallow, and that this quick success has overlooked the key and more important principles of life.

> I am not suggesting that elements of the Personality Ethic...are not beneficial, in fact sometimes essential for success. I believe they are. But these are secondary, not primary traits. Perhaps, in utilizing our human capacity to build on the foundation of generations before us, we have inadvertently become so focused on our own building that we have forgotten the foundation that holds it up.[7]

No wonder Madonna fell into the trap of reinvention that she resides in to this day. Her success seemed entirely dependent on maintaining her public image. It is missing the foundation, which makes me wonder: have we become completely dependent on the opinions of others to determine not only our success but our self-worth?

Society's view of success is based on a false identity, or what is outwardly visible. We have internalized that measurement and applied it daily to how we show up and establish our self-worth in our spheres of influence.

What others see on the outside is often what we believe determines our true standing in the world.

And if we ever try to break free from this limiting belief, reinforcement is just a few scrolls or swipes away. An overwhelming amount of our societal pressure today is created by the warped perception of reality on social media, causing us to collectively lose our grip on what's real. Our eyes spend hours spectating lives that aren't ours, all the while doing little to improve our own situations.

This twisted reality isn't going anywhere. Quite the opposite. The influencer marketing industry is expected to surpass $16.4 billion in 2022.[8] It makes sense then that global, self-proclaimed influencer Kim Kardashian was asked in 2021 to host the long-running sketch show *Saturday Night Live*.

During her opening monologue, Kardashian called out her global clout. "I'm so used to having 360 million followers watching my every move, and how many people watch SNL, like ten million? Tonight is just a chill, intimate night for me."

While not all influencers have their tweets read by millions, it has become widely known that one path to money, power, and fame is to promote a shiny life online. In only a handful of years and with the magic of algorithms, influencers have made a level playing field with those we formerly considered actual celebrities. They are rewarded with profit because they are successful at knowing what their audience likes and delivering it daily.

We may not all be influencers, but we all have been guilty of posting pictures to make our lives look more extraordinary. Our pictures tell a story. Most of the time, they are just a highlight reel. And part of that is because excitement is more marketable, so it's what you and I hear about most often. But the unhealthy part is that many are striving for the wrong reasons: to prove they are somebody special. Nobody wants to be mediocre and uninteresting.

MERITOCRACY MYTH

Meritocracy, a system where success is defined by your merit or achievements, has become the leading ideal in our society. The rungs of the ladder are set before us, and those who can achieve them—via good grades, prestigious college, an impressive job title—are deemed successful. It seems the door is open to all, but upon closer inspection, we find it is not. The system of meritocracy is flawed and ends up swallowing us rather than helping us to fly. Ironically, we can become lost even if we do achieve.

In his book *The Second Mountain*, bestselling author and commentator David Brooks addresses the insecure overachiever. He describes a spiritual or mental state called *acedia*.

> Acedia is the quieting of passion. It is a lack of care. It is living a life that doesn't arouse your strong passions and therefore instills a sluggishness of the soul, like an oven set on warm. The person living in acedia may have a job and a family, but he is not entirely grabbed by his own life. His heart is over there, but his life is over here... the meritocracy encourages you to drift into a life that society loves but which you don't.[9]

While Madonna's drive to prove she *is* somebody is relatable, it's also exhausting. The greatest fear of many of my clients, especially those in leadership roles, is not having the power or the title anymore.

Even for me, walking away from that status and all that came with my job was a test for my ego. It was a difficult transition not to be Traci Barrett, HGTV executive, anymore. To this day, ten years after having left HGTV, the vast majority of my friends *still* introduce me as Traci-who-used-to-work-for-HGTV. It's still my claim to fame, and while I know it's interesting and I love talking about it, that success is behind me now. I don't want to be defined by something that's now well in my past. I also don't want to be defined by one thing.

Don't get me wrong; I am just as guilty of doing this myself. If I'm feeling insignificant or unknown, sometimes I can find myself saying, "Oh yeah, well, I used to work for HGTV . . ." And that gets people interested in me again. It's human nature, but it's also a trap to define my self-worth and ultimately my significance in something shiny, glamorous, extraordinary, and fleeting.

When I look back and think about what I miss about those days besides the fun and the people, it may be the public recognition. Whether it was for the work I did or for the network I was a part of building. The pride and glory you feel when you are widely admired or publicly recognized is real. It feels good. I miss it. Who wouldn't?

This is the ultimate battle: the battle of self. I'm conditioned to promote myself, recognize myself, elevate myself. Deprogramming this conditioning is no easy task. It does not mean I can't feel good about myself or my achievements, but it does mean I am no longer committed to them as the ultimate definition of who I am.

The more courageous thing for me to do is to properly honor those achievements but then move on and choose a new path, like the one of Mother Teresa. Be extraordinarily significant in the most ordinary ways. Become significant by walking the path of life, one foot in front of the other, impacting the road ahead step by step, choice by choice, action by action. But how do I learn how to do that in a way that is unique and fulfilling to me? How do I find my way to significance?

> *"People that know they are important, think about others. People that think they are important, think about themselves."*
>
> **—HANS F. HANSEN**

THREE QUESTIONS AT THE CROSSROADS

If you want to get anywhere effectively and efficiently, you must know your current location and desired destination. The next step is to map out your route. To get to the top of the pyramid of your human need for self-actualization, you must courageously commit to answering some key questions that will not only continually shape your worldview but also help you create a map to the life you want. The key questions are these: How Did I Get Here?, Why Do I Exist?, and Where Am I Going?

How Did I Get Here?

When we don't understand our story fully and completely from beginning to end, we lose the ability to find meaning in life. When we look back, we often highlight the failures of omission, those things we didn't do, and the failures of commission, those things we regret we did. We can sit in those regrets, wishing life had been different, and become unable to let go of the pain, trauma, or anger.

Other times we can look back and see only the best moments of life, and hold youth up too high, believing the best years are behind us.

Our past should not define us, nor should our present situation hold us back.

The power comes in looking at your entire life as a story. Maybe how you got to where you are today is a little fuzzy or seemed like what was expected of you, but you are still the hero of your story. All the triumphs and trials, successes and failures are yours to own and learn from. Moving forward, the unwritten chapters are yours to design. Understanding this allows you to move from passive living to active living.

In our stories we are able to see ourselves in the third person. We can analyze the big picture story of our lives and recognize our belief patterns, value systems, and imposed expectations.

I had a lot of power and control in my job, but there were often times when, left alone with my thoughts, I felt lost. I couldn't quite understand why. I've come to realize that maybe it wasn't the job at all. Maybe it was the culmination of how I was being measured and how I had spent my entire life measuring myself. Within a compartmentalized perspective, I didn't understand what it was all for, *sans* the money. I didn't know the purpose. If only I could have pushed past the success and understood my significance.

In the pages ahead, you are going to explore how the major

events and pivotal points in your story may be shaping your worldview today. Is your life experience holding you back from seeing the world around you as it really is? Are you seeing the world as you are or hope to be?

Why Do I Exist?

Why do we have so much trouble articulating the answer to this? We all have some surface idea of who we are—some combination of our qualities, beliefs, personality, likes, and dislikes. But we have trouble answering the real *who* of who we are and the real *why* of why we are here.

Bestselling author Simon Sinek is well known for sharing a powerful model of business leadership. In his book *Start with Why,* he stresses the importance of how leaders need to not only find the *why* of their company but always keep it front and center if they want to achieve and maintain success. He explains:

> Every company, organization or group with the ability to inspire starts with a person or small group of people who were inspired to do something bigger than themselves. Gaining clarity of WHY, ironically, is not the hard part. It is the discipline to trust one's gut, to stay true to one's purpose, cause or beliefs. Remaining completely in balance and authentic is the most difficult part.[10]

If I were to tie HGTV's success to one thing, it would be the leadership's ability to keep focus on our mission, our why. When you are starting a television network, one of the hardest parts of development is having enough programming to fill twenty-four hours a day. For HGTV, we were creating a network whose stated mission was to provide home and garden programming that was filled with ideas, information, and inspiration. This was a lofty mission but one that excited the team and gave us drive.

The problem was there wasn't that much home and garden programming in existence in 1994. We didn't have enough money to lure Martha Stewart our way, and the programs we could acquire were dry and dated.

Piecing together a full programming slate over the years was always a tall hill to climb. While the programming team did an excellent job going out and finding fresh, new talent, there was always the temptation to run syndicated sitcoms such as *Home Improvement* or *The Golden Girls* or movie reruns. Not only would programs like this help fill programming hours, it would also guarantee easy advertising dollars. The only problem was these shows had absolutely nothing to do with our mission.

When you are a fledgling network in need of eyeballs, ideas like these can feel too hard to pass up. Thankfully, the team resisted, and we continually moved forward with our commitment to stay true to our goal. Would running *Home Improvement* have turned off viewers? Maybe not. But it most likely would have derailed our team. We would have begun to stretch ourselves outside our mission and made excuses to take programming just to keep the lights on. I believe HGTV could have gone the route of many other television networks and been a collection of varying shows with no consistent theme.

The whys of our companies and the whys of our life are threads that hold the fabric of everything else together. When we keep them front and center, we may need to make sacrifices in the short run, but in the long run, our impact will be clear and inspiring.

I believe that finding and keeping your WHY ensures that you are crafting the life you want rather than settling for a life that comes your way. You are more aware of what is meant for you, and you don't miss out on the opportunities that are aligned to your personal mission.

On the flip side, you don't have a fear of missing out on things that aren't good for you. You can distinguish the difference and see that some opportunities are best for others. You don't find worth in the number of things you do or accomplish but rather in your purpose and design. You become grateful for how you were uniquely created and are excited for living out the distinctive purpose given to you through your talents, passions, and values.

Your life has to be built on something. Everyone has a "why" behind their "should." It is your "therefore." I am this, therefore I should do that. Our whys are the roots to our behaviors, choices, and actions. In the pages ahead, you will learn how to discover your why and craft a mission statement that will serve as your filter for building a life of significance.

Where Am I Going?

In my coaching, I find that people at a midlife crossroads often feel more dissatisfied than depressed. Overachievers may feel fear, as lacking a clear goal to work toward is unfamiliar and uncomfortable territory for them. They are uneasy now that they've surpassed the predetermined mile markers and are left panting at the beginning of an unpaved road.

Rites of passage have faded, and an uncertainty has seeped in. Except now our habits, good and bad, and comforts we enjoy are driven so deep that turning the ship to a new horizon seems riskier than staying the course.

Elizabeth Gilbert, author of the 2006 memoir *Eat, Pray, Love*, faced this dilemma long before midlife. "It's exceedingly likely that my greatest success is behind me," said Gilbert in a 2009 TED Talk.[11] Her book sold over ten million copies, was translated into more than thirty languages, made it into Oprah's Book Club, and remained on the *New York Times* Best Seller list for 187 weeks.

And if there was any doubt that she had reached the top, Julia Roberts played her in the movie version, with Javier Bardem as her love interest. Gilbert was living every author's wildest dream by achieving society's widely viewed and agreed-upon definition of success. Gilbert found herself face-to-face with the stark reality that the peak of her career may already have been behind her at the ripe old age of thirty-seven. So now what? What was Gilbert going to do so as not to be defined by that singular book for the rest of her life?

Of course, *Eat, Pray, Love* was a big break for her career. But it left her in a tricky position moving forward as an author trying to figure out how she was ever again going to write a book that would exceed or even meet expectations. She considered quitting, but that would mean losing her beloved vocation. All Gilbert had ever wanted her entire life was to be an author. She knew the task at hand was to discover a way to find the inspiration to write the next book regardless of its inevitable less-than-blockbuster outcome. "In other words," she says, "I had to find a way to make sure that my creativity survived its own success."

I have grappled with this myself. To this day, many colleagues in my industry don't understand why I left HGTV. There are times when I find myself feeling nostalgic or romanticizing my time at HGTV. Looking back, there was a lot of greatness (and wildly fulfilling amounts of glamour and fun), but here is what I can say with certainty now: HGTV may have been the pinnacle of my success, but it wasn't the pinnacle of my significance.

In the pages ahead, you will discover how to look at your life from a 360-degree perspective allowing you to articulate a clear and achievable vision for your future.

THE QUEST FOR SIGNIFICANCE

Answering these questions for myself turned out to be a reintroduction of me to me. It has been and continues to be a journey to discovering a new way to be valued and to value others. While having a highly successful career has its obvious rewards to society, it is important to recognize that having a life of significance provides deeper and more lasting benefits.

The biggest reward of a life of significance is becoming a better version of yourself—which in turn leads to experiencing better health, wealth, and relationships.

Better You

The best version of yourself is when you are deeply aware of your unique gifts and have committed to living out your purpose to impact the world around you. You are a person committed to becoming wiser by setting aside self-centeredness and embracing self-awareness. You are a person who has designed a map to get to your ultimate vision. Going on this journey—and truly enjoying it—is an invitation to a better you.

Better Health

A life of significance is a life of balance. When we are committed to an intentional life, we understand the need to put on our oxygen mask first. We know that rest, refueling, space, and time are key ingredients to physical, mental, intellectual, and spiritual health. It is in that space and rest where we find ourselves, restore our health, and recommit to our strategic plan for a significant life.

Better Wealth

One of the most gratifying rewards of living a life of significance is turning a career into a calling. Once you can define your purpose in a clear and actionable way, your vocation is no longer a means to an end. Rather, it becomes an avenue to living out your daily mission in life and realizing your true talents and passions. While more money doesn't ensure happiness, doing what you love with purpose will more than likely bring you a rich life.

Better Relationships

You might think that spending so much time working to answer such deep questions about yourself will lead to even more self-centeredness and individualism. The hope is that the opposite will be true. Going deep and answering these key questions helps you release your insecurities, which will ultimately draw you away from yourself and toward others. As we discover our own truth, we are pushed in the direction of love instead of fear. As our path becomes more deeply rooted in humility, we long to reconnect and deepen our relationships with those around us. Therein lies the hope.

Ultimately, the quest for significance leads us to a life of greater love—love for ourselves and love for others. If we all woke up and committed to a brighter tomorrow—one of intention, purpose, and connection—we could push our sections of the world a bit closer together. Love trumps fear. Love repairs, restores, and binds. But love must be realized and pursued. A life of significance illuminates the way.

A STRATEGIC PLAN FOR YOUR LIFE

A life of significance is one that has meaning and purpose. But like anything worthwhile, it takes effort. It takes a plan. A strategic plan.

To go someplace you've never been, you need a map. A strategic map for your life is not some revolutionary idea. Strategic planning has been around for millennia. Almost every business executive has experienced some form of it in an effort to optimize their business. But far fewer of us have considered it as a tool to use for our life, which should have us all scratching our heads and asking, "Why not?"

Strategically mapping out your business, if done correctly, brings clarity, focus, and a path to a more profitable bottom line. A strategic map for your life, if done correctly, can bring clarity to who you are, focus on the right vision for the future, and a path to a more robust and positive impact to the world around you.

It is essential to make sure you have the correct perspective prior to jumping into such an important process. Changing from the inside first is imperative if you hope for external success. It sounds simple, but this is the hardest part. You must start with the self-awareness gained by understanding what got you where you are today. In the chapters that follow, you will have an opportunity to look at your story and the patterns you've developed along the way. While it's true some of those patterns have gotten you to where you are, it's also true that many are standing in the way of your most fruitful future. In order to move forward, let's first go backward.

Reflections

- What questions are you wrestling with today?
- What do you feel you need more clarity on?
- What drives you to get out of bed in the morning?
- How would you define a life of significance?

CHAPTER THREE

YOUR STORY

"To understand how things are going to end you must know how things began."

—PETER PAN

I was twenty-eight years old. I felt great. I was rising up the corporate ladder at HGTV, building a new company with a team of people I loved, dating the man who would eventually become my future husband, and enjoying life in the big city of Chicago. I felt like I had made it. But making it was taking its toll. I was often burning the candle at both ends and pushing down a lot of stress, but hey, I'll sleep when I die, right? Then one morning, as it does, life threw me a curveball.

When I woke up, I immediately knew something was wrong. My hands and feet felt like they were on fire. My head felt foggy and sluggish. I had trouble getting out of bed and ended up on my hands and knees in tears. I called in sick and went to see my doctor. After an exam and blood work, he came in to tell me the bad news. I had rheumatoid arthritis. It was an incurable disease that would progress if I didn't start a medication regime immediately.

I explained to him that there must be some sort of mistake as I was not eighty-two years old. He explained that it wasn't that type of arthritis. In his experience, RA surfaced in most people between the ages of twenty-seven and thirty-two. This was an autoimmune disease, and my body was attacking itself.

I sat stunned and confused. This was not in my plan. I needed my body and energy to keep the achievement going. The thought of dealing with this unwelcome hurdle was unimaginable and inconvenient, to say the least.

As I worked to find a quick solution, I kept my diagnosis to myself. My younger sister, a gifted nurse, did extensive research and flew to Chicago to be by my side. After discouraging visits with rheumatologists who wanted to start an aggressive steroid treatment, I landed on a more integrative medical approach. I changed my diet dramatically, adding mindfulness techniques such as yoga and meditation to my routine, and started taking low-dose medications.

Miraculously, after many months, I was able to get my disease under control, but my life was forever altered. I had to care for myself differently and would have both good days and bad for years to come.

For those first several years I felt flawed and embarrassed. I found it incredibly hard to tell anyone I had RA. I just couldn't get the words out of my mouth. Not only did saying it out loud make it real, but I felt it would paint me in a new way to friends, family, and colleagues. I shuddered internally at the thought of seeming wounded, less than, weak. For the first time in my life, I found myself swimming in a world of self-doubt without the ability to get myself to shore. Why was my body defying me?

What I eventually found was that it was more than just a body issue; it was a mind issue. There was something inside me that was wholeheartedly rejecting the idea of being seen as sick or somehow disabled. I became mortified by the thought that people would label me as someone with a chronic illness. What was it in my story that made me react this way?

I had achieved so much in life. Kept control. Manifested what I believed should be my destiny. Now I was powerless. I could lessen my symptoms, but I couldn't cure the disease. I couldn't conquer and achieve this new wrinkle in my story.

I was staring at this unwelcomed event in my life with mostly anger, resentment, and fear. It wouldn't be until I was able to look at it with grace and kindness that it found a better place in my story.

THE NARRATOR OF YOUR STORY

You can't build a life you want without accepting the life you have. Without looking at the highs and lows of your story thus far, you can miss understanding the choices you've made and the dreams you've deferred. That perpetual misunderstanding can lead to repeating the same cycles of stuckness.

While the idea of going back in order to move forward might seem overwhelming or a waste of time, it is the perspective we gain in this significant step that propels us toward a future of significance. In this chapter we will begin to make peace with—and even appreciate—the foundation of the life we have so that we can confidently craft the life we want. We must come to honor our life experience, for without all of it we would not be who we are and where we are today.

The only path to the future is through the past. Or, as one of the first existentialist philosophers, Søren Kierkegaard, famously wrote, "Life can only be understood backwards, but it must be lived forwards."

Dan McAdams, author and professor of psychology at Northwestern University, writes that humans find meaning and create our identities through the stories we tell of our lives.

McAdams discusses three aspects of the self that people display in their story of life. He describes people first as "actors" pretty much from birth. We have personality traits, interact with the world, and have roles to play. As we get old enough to have goals, we then become "agents"—still playing our roles and interacting with the world, but making decisions with the hopes of producing desired outcomes. The third and final aspect is "author," when we begin to bundle ideas about the future with experiences from the past and present to form a narrative self.

> The stories we make and tell about the major transitions in our own lives contribute to our identities, help us cope with challenges and stress, shape how we see the future, and help to determine the nature of our interpersonal relationships and our unique positionings in the social and cultural world.[12]

As we age, we become authors and narrators of our stories. When we talk to each other about events of the day or the years past, we tell it in a narrative form. Even when we remember it in the corners of our mind, our memories are our stories. We weave together the facts, events, and moments to create who we are and the world in which we live.

UNLOCKING YOUR STORY

> *"Those who fail to learn from history are doomed to repeat it."*
>
> **—WINSTON CHURCHILL**

Too often people try to plan the future without gaining the necessary clarity, understanding, and acceptance of the story of their life. To their disappointment, their future goals remain unrealized as their life stays stationary for the same reasons it always has. Unfortunately, they aren't unaware or haven't confronted those reasons and dealt with them in a way that will unlock the door to their future.

Why don't we take the time to look back when doing so means gaining a brighter future? Typically, it is a fear of losing control. We hold on to the reins so tightly to keep ourselves from feeling pain or from facing the truth of how we see ourselves or how others may see us.

Another reason we try to forget the events of the past and how they impacted us is that being still and knowing ourselves can be challenging. We must travel through our history and allow adequate space to recognize patterns, scripts, fears, and even unrealized hopes. This heightened awareness helps connect the dots to what propelled our success up to today and what may be holding us back from making the leap toward the life we want.

The longer we carry the untruths, the traumas, the incorrect scripts, the lies, and the fears in our life, the worse they become. As we age, those small untruths become boulders in our path, too massive to go around, so we stay stuck. Being stuck is such an awful feeling. But one thing I know for sure is the boulders in your life may be large, but if you dare to work through them, they are moveable.

As Brené Brown says, "When we imprison our hearts to protect our egos, we kill courage. Yes, a liberated heart is more vulnerable, but it's also more daring." [13] Let's dare to tell the whole story.

STORY PIVOT POINTS

"If history were taught in the form of stories, it would never be forgotten."

—RUDYARD KIPLING

Human beings form their worldview through life experience and most often through early childhood development. We can change our view for the better, but first we must recognize the frameworks we have created for ourselves. The easiest way to begin to recognize our frameworks is to consider all the major pivot points of our life.

Story pivot points are events in your life that have altered the course of your journey. These altering moments of life could be a choice you made or something you had no control over. They could be something done to you or something you did. You could perceive the pivot point as a positive moment or a negative one. They could be big or small, but they made a significant change. Story pivot points are not merely events in your life, but they are important milestones that changed the trajectory of your life story.

As author Napoleon Hill puts it, "It is strange, but true, that the most important turning-points of life often come at the most unexpected times and in the most unexpected ways."

Some various examples of story pivot points could be a marriage or divorce, the birth of your first child, an unwelcome diagnosis, a special teacher who intervened at a key moment, making that winning basket or scoring the lead in the high school play, getting that first key job or getting fired, taking a perspective-changing trip abroad, a relationship-breaking argument with a sibling, the death of a loved one, abuse at the hands of a predator, or getting sober.

Many of us are grateful for parts of our past but cringe at other memories. Whether we can't shake the regret from a poor choice or the anger and bitterness from bad things that have been done to us, there is a lot we bury amid looking back. Without true acceptance of our whole story—the good and the bad—it is hard to fully understand who we are or truly embrace the person we are meant to be in the future.

Many of us have lived lives shaped by the desire to succeed, achieve, or gain approval. Along the way things have happened to us. We either process them and learn, cling to them and never let them go, or bury them deep inside, hoping they never show their awful face again. We build walls to protect ourselves from fears, insecurities, and traumas. These walls protect us from the pain by putting some distance between us and the pieces we'd rather leave behind. But the wall also creates a barrier to our soul and can cast shade on our true desires, passions, and longings.

We often move from accomplishment to accomplishment, leaving little space to connect to the whispers of our heart or recognize our inner voice. Our drive to achieve, be responsible, maintain our image, and be loved can keep us so firmly planted in the whirlwind of it all that we appear to be sleepwalking through life. We dream of sabbaticals, vacations, or winning the lottery. Those dreams convey our soul's craving for space, time, and rest as our mind desires to awaken.

To awaken our minds and connect wholeheartedly to our souls, we must truly understand how we got to where we are today, recognizing each pivotal turning point as a moment that shaped and molded us into the beautiful people we are today.

The Benefits of Assessing the Past

Life can be the best teacher if we let it. If we stop and recognize the pivot points or stare at them long enough, the dots connect, and our feelings toward the hardest ones can change. We can come to appreciate and have grace toward those particular moments and through that grace find freedom and acceptance of who we've become. Our vulnerability in going there can be the key to moving forward.

> *"Life is 10 percent what happens to you and 90 percent how you react to it."*
>
> **—CHARLES R. SWINDOLL**

The goal is not for you to sit in your past and ruminate for extended periods of time like we might in therapy, but rather to walk through your past, recognize each pivot point, articulate it, and keep it moving.

Often you are able to see repeated patterns and their causes, sometimes for the very first time in your adult life. You bring the root of behaviors and beliefs out into the light. As you look at each pivotal point, ask the following: What happened? Why did it happen? How did it affect you? How are you carrying it forward into today?

Throughout any life story there are ups and downs, peaks, and valleys. These catalysts are the making of the pivotal moments of our lives.

The Peaks of Life

Every story has its moments of excitement and joy. These peaks of life often give us hope, build our self-esteem, and open our eyes to how we may be uniquely gifted.

The key events that fill you with pride or happiness don't have to be major or even something others in your life remember. The only important thing is that you remember those positive, pivotal moments and keep them close to your heart.

Peaks also include those people in your life who leaned into knowing you more, loving you more, or helping you become a better person.

One of my clients described growing up in a quiet, uneventful home. He suffered from undiagnosed dyslexia and often saw himself as less than the students around him. While he did okay in school, he struggled to see himself as any different or unique from what he deemed the average Joe. Through the encouragement of his father, he decided to go from shooting hoops in the driveway to trying out for his high school basketball team. Once on the team, he realized that with a little effort he might be able to shine. Practicing every weekend and leaning into the wisdom of his coaches, he became a better basketball player with each game. On the night of the big game against the school's archrival, he hit the winning basket. This night became a pivotal turning point for him. It solidified in his mind that he does have unique talents and with effort and belief in himself, he can hone and grow those talents into winning moments. This pivot point altered his journey and was one of the key factors that gave him the courage to ultimately start his own company and lead it to success.

Each one of our positive pivotal moments connects to another. Over time, it sharpens the lens through which we see ourselves and our place in the world. If we recognize those moments and build upon them, we begin to shape a character that can impact others.

As we pull out those memories and examine the effect they had on our lives, we can more clearly define the beliefs they formed in our minds. Those beliefs shape how we make decisions today. Those moments created consequences for our lives. Moving forward, our deeper understanding of them can produce even larger reverberations for our future.

And the Valleys . . .

When you are driving in a rainstorm, you know it will take you longer to get to your destination. The same is true with storms of life; they typically slow you down or may even stop you in your tracks. Suddenly life isn't normal anymore. You end up in a valley. Even if you had a relatively easy childhood and amazing parents, you have certainly wound up in a valley once or twice in your life.

Often our darkest valleys create wounds. These wounds have shaped many of our beliefs, attitudes, and behaviors. For some of us the storms of life have made us better friends and partners. For others we keep tripping over the same issues, and our relationships are unable to thrive.

The exercise of looking back and understanding more deeply the elements of the negative experiences in our lives is an opportunity to uncover unresolved emotions or unhealthy patterns of behavior. To design a more impactful future, we need to do the work to unlock a better version of ourselves. Losses can be gains if they wake us up to something new. As Helen Keller once said, "Character cannot be developed in ease and quiet. Only through experience of trial and suffering can the soul be strengthened, ambition inspired, and success achieved."

One of my clients suffered a dangerous illness, leaving him in the hospital ICU for over three months. He came out the other side with a long road of recovery ahead of him. While he told me the story, his breathing was still labored and his limbs still weak. He shared with me his newfound gratitude for life. He had decided to quit his job and start the entrepreneurial endeavor he had been dreaming of for years. His face glowed as he looked toward what he perceived as a brighter future. He didn't downplay the hardship of his journey, but he was able to give meaning to it. By contrast, his wife had become bitter. She resented the fact that he had gotten sick. She couldn't understand why it had to happen to them. She was angry that more friends and family hadn't come to her aid during the strenuous time. She now lamented the time wasted in the hospital and seemed annoyed with the recovery process that was ahead of them.

There is an old saying: "The same sun that melts wax hardens clay." In other words, the same experience that softens and grows one's heart can harden and embitter another's.

Your time in a valley may cause you to curve into yourself and become smaller, or it can cause you to step into a bigger version of yourself, emerging on the other side more resilient.

Looking at your past can help you recognize negative pivot points of your own making. The idols we have created in our lives—the things that we worship and therefore have ownership over us—can often grab us by the throat. Humans tend to gravitate toward worshiping something. It is good to examine what might have a hold on you as the grip can bring havoc into our lives. It could be work, your love life, your possessions, your money, your children, or something else that has the title to your heart. If anything goes wrong with that thing, your heart implodes and becomes devastated.

Oftentimes successful people struggle with this loss of control rather intensely, and it can lead to explosive emotions, creating bigger storms in our life than had we let things run their course. Looking at self-inflicted pain is often the hardest exercise but a necessary one in order to break the pattern in the future.

Some storms in life were not at all your doing. Terrible things can be done to us, often during childhood, when we are too young to understand or have control. Some of us grew up in unsafe environments, lived in poverty, had authority figures who criticized or shamed us, or were neglected or abandoned. These horrific circumstances can seem unfair and agonizing when looking back. Sometimes we can piece together meaning, but we may go our entire lives and never know why that had to happen to us. Furthermore, these events can leave us with some rather disturbing beliefs about ourselves and the world around us.

Some people sit in that storm their entire lives, unable to move forward. They live a life trapped in anguish. It may not be on their surface, but the iceberg is deep beneath the waterline.

Terrible things are terrible. We can't change that, nor should we try to downplay them by always finding a silver lining. We also don't want to spend time placing blame. Instead, acknowledging, articulating, and examining it long enough will allow us to effectively connect the dots. Seeing the impact this event had on our life today will allow us to weather the storm well and come out the other side better rather than bitter.

The goal of walking through the past valleys is to wake us up to a new way of looking at them. Most people think negative input equals a negative output. While it is true we can be left with negative thoughts, beliefs, and feelings from these moments in our life, it can also be true that with reexamination and renewed perspective, we can change a negative output to a positive one.

Learning how to navigate the valleys can bring you much joy. Rather than striving to avoid pain, you can live with freedom knowing that if you fall or fail, you will survive. It is the attitude with which you process your storms that determines the effect they will have on you in the future.

How do you deal with the ups and downs of your life today? As a full-grown but still-growing adult looking back, what is your attitude toward the negative experiences of your life?

THE ROAD TO GREATER SIGNIFICANCE

Your story may likely have several pivotal points that are connected to various achievements. Becoming valedictorian, captain of the football team, or recognized at a gymnastics tournament gave us a taste of what it felt like to be admired and affirmed, and we felt good about ourselves. These points started to shape what it feels like to find worth.

As children, when we are recognized for accomplishing something, it releases endorphins, dopamine, and serotonin in our brain and gives us a happy feeling that we try to keep as long as possible.[14] These wins are typically tied to things we are good at, ways we have pleased others, or a task we have completed. We become conditioned at a young age to do good so we can experience this lovely feeling of success. Sometimes the successes are simply experiences that have altered our worldview. They can be trips we have taken to other places outside our normal environment or ways we have served our community through charitable work. These experiences also release the same chemicals in our brains and leave a lasting mark in our story.

For many business owners, you can see those early pioneering activities they did as a kid, whether it was the paper route, the lemonade stand, or the little lawn care business they started. You can see it at a very young age. You can see how those events shaped their future life as entrepreneurs through the sense of worth they felt for earning that first five dollars for mowing the lawn.

As we grow up, those successes can be more significant and surprisingly can hold us back at midlife crossroads. As people look back at their accomplishments, the repeated phrases are often "those were the best years of my life," "oh, to be young again," "I'll never have another (fill in the blank) like that," and "I wish I could be like that again." These statements or beliefs are seeds of resignation in our minds. They make us feel like the years ahead couldn't possibly measure up to the years behind us.

I fell easily into this trap. Even as I began to build a new business and shaped new opportunities to walk alongside people as a coach and leadership strategist, I would whisper to myself that this was just a nice little side project. I would never achieve the level of success, prestige, or salary that I had experienced at HGTV. *Those days are behind me. Whatever the future holds for me, it will pale in comparison to what I experienced in my earlier decades.*

Not only was this limiting belief of my past success not helpful, it was also not true. While I may not experience the shiny high-profile success that HGTV brought my way, I can distinctly feel that I am firmly on my road to greater significance.

A friend once said to me, "What if your time at HGTV was just a stepping stone to what you are doing today? What if your real purpose and fulfillment comes through what you are doing now?"

It hadn't occurred to me that this was an option. It was as if I had put myself on a shelf—like a relic collecting dust. My past could be admired, but my future was simply a time of going through the motions. Suddenly, my view shifted. I no longer look at my past successes as the be-all and end-all, but rather as pivotal moments that have added to who I am today. They are experiences that have shaped me, and if I am intentional, I can continue to add exceptional experiences into my future as I build a second half of life filled with significance.

I find that I can hold on to my successes too tightly. I can mistakenly think that if they shine brighter, my imperfections will be less evident. Success can feel safer. Our ego likes to rest in the safety of accomplishment. But this can make it hard for other people to connect with or relate to me. My deepest connection with other humans will not come through their admiration for my achievements but for my authenticity in my more vulnerable moments. When I accept this truth, I can see my successes for what they are: lovely and beautiful moments in my life. That's it. They don't define me, own me, or determine my future. I can look on them admirably and be proud. They may make my life easier in some ways, and that is marvelous, but if I let them define or own me, the good can turn and hinder my growth.

Taking your stories from success to significance means creating a new arc that requires a shift from a focus on self to a connection to others. Why remedy your negative patterns or beliefs? Why renew your perspective through new learnings? Because if you want to ensure that the last chapters of your story bring fulfillment, meaning, and impact, you must create this new story arc.

BEAUTY IN THE CRACKS

The Japanese art of repairing broken pottery with powdered gold, silver, or platinum lacquer is known as *kintsugi*, or *kintsukuroi*, meaning "golden joinery" or "golden repair." This philosophy treats breakage and repair as part of the history of an object rather than something to disguise. The cracks and repairs are simply an event in the life of an object, not the end of the object. It's an invitation to embrace the flawed or imperfect, and this is the ideal context for how to address your past.

Kintsugi has also been related to the Japanese philosophy of *mushin* or "no mind," which encompasses the concepts of non-attachment, acceptance of change, and fate. Not only is there no attempt to hide the damage, but the repair is literally illuminated, made more beautiful and even coveted as a result. *Mushin* embodies a premise of fully existing within the moment and of equanimity amid changing conditions.[15] Over time, the vicissitudes of our lives start to show. While the breaks, knicks, and shattering are visible in a repaired piece of pottery, human cracks aren't always as easy to see.

I love this approach of looking at our past as a form of golden repair. We must gain perspective on the past before we can ever live fully in our present or begin dreaming big for our future. Your past shapes the way you see and believe in yourself. It even shapes how you act and react in any given moment. It shapes the scripts you recite in your head each and every day. It can shape your emotional intelligence and your behavior toward others. Unpacking the past and seeing your life for all of its good and bad is a powerful and necessary part of a life-mapping process. When done well, you can see your life as a Japanese *kintsugi* vase: a beautiful piece of art.

This is easier said than done because as we age, our natural inclination leads us to become masters at covering up the cracks and imperfections. Whether we cover the exterior with cosmetic alterations or hide the interior with inauthentic armor, we become forgery artists. We create an imitation rather than keep the original in all its glory. What we don't realize is that the imitation is much more fragile and weak. It is the vase with the cracks exposed in full view that is the one that withstands the storms and grows mature in wisdom.

It's hard to live a more intentional life without entering into complete self-awareness. It's hard for others to trust our motives if we haven't done the work of getting ourselves to a better place. To get to a place where we see our past as a work of art, we must lift the veil on the places we've been and see them from start to finish in a new light.

Seeing my story in its entirety, peaks and valleys, successes and failures, not only helped me to appreciate more fully where I am today but also helped me uncover the influences, beliefs, and labels I needed to rewrite in order to end unwanted cycles. In the following chapter, we will unearth the underlying and unhealthy patterns in our story that are standing between the life we have and the life we want.

Reflections

- What are the key pivotal points of your life story?
- As you look over your list of positive and negative pivotal points in your life, how did each alter the trajectory of how you got to where you are today?

CHAPTER FOUR

YOUR PATTERNS

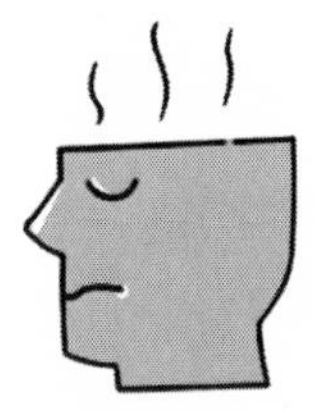

"Tomorrow hopes we have learned something from yesterday."

—JOHN WAYNE

Groundhog Day is one of my favorite movies not only because it makes me laugh out loud but because I see it as a bit of a masterclass on how to change your life. Salty and narcissistic Phil Connors, played by Bill Murray, is faced with reliving the same day over and over again. Trapped in this new reality, he is eventually pulled out of his autopilot way of living and forced to see his life and those around him in a new way. He finally embraces a new mindset and leans into literally making each day better than the last. Ultimately, he breaks his negative personal patterns and unlocks a new version of himself that, in the end, endears him to others and transports him to a better life.

Successful, driven people tend to spend a great deal of their time each day focused on the outside world, solving external problems with speed and ingenuity. Rarely stopping to take a breath, they maneuver from one activity to another.

When strategically planning for your life, you must pause and examine the world within. Looking at life through the lens of your inner thoughts and character can enable you to connect the dots of the common patterns and themes that direct your actions and behaviors.

Sometimes I wonder what it would be like to wake up to the same day over and over. Facing myself in every interaction with such focus and presence. Honestly, I shudder at the thought. I know there would be moments where I would be unhappy with how I showed up, what I said, and how little I may have paid attention. But I also know that I'd work hard to correct myself and make the next day better. Much like Phil in *Groundhog Day*, we must awaken ourselves from our focus on the external and begin to examine our daily lives with an internal focus.

THE STORY WE WANT TO TELL

Without mining for positive meaning within our life stories, we can end up in a never-ending cycle of mental and emotional suffering.

One of my most crucial tasks as a trained counselor and executive coach is to help my clients retell their story in a more constructive or forward-looking way. It is through this revelatory retelling that they are able to better interpret their journey and, in turn, edit their narrative in an empowering way that gives it meaning. Once they are able to fully shape a positive story of their life, they can alter their behaviors for the better and discover greater purpose moving forward.

Once upon a time... we were all born with a human need to love and be loved. In childhood, as helpless creatures, we bond with our caregivers, which for most of us is at least one of our parents. We are highly attuned to how we can best please or connect with them. Over time, these interactions and exchanges cultivate patterns of feeling, thinking, and believing. Some are helpful but many are unhelpful because no matter how loved we were, our parents weren't perfect. They had their own mix of healthy and unhealthy patterns imprinted on them in childhood.

All of us have had lives filled with opinions, judgments, toxic words, bad habits, and a whole lot of noise in our heads. We also learned behaviors as kids to survive the chaos of our family, home environment, or cultural interactions in the world. Those behaviors don't tend to serve us well as adults. They can even turn to blind spots that hinder our relationships, especially those in the workplace.

Our patterns and behaviors inform how we tell our stories throughout our lives. In our retelling we can hear whether we believe ourselves lovable or not, successful or lucky, wounded or healed, purposeful or lost. The patterns we pick up in childhood are reinforced during the pivotal points of our lives, often showing up as unhelpful behaviors or beliefs. Recognizing the patterns that flow through the chapters of our story and shape our identity is a key step in rooting out what is holding us back today.

RECOGNIZING YOUR PATTERNS

> *"You can't heal what you don't acknowledge."*
>
> **—JACK CANFIELD**

Having the proper perspective as you become the executive editor of your story can be the impetus to reshaping your character for the better, which is imperative to leading a more significant life.

Ultimately, to design the life you want, you must first heal and reshape your story up to this point. Recognizing and rescripting your personal patterns will allow you to grow in a way that enables you to have more gratifying and impactful chapters ahead.

Reflecting on all the pivotal moments of your life story, both good and bad, how do you view your story? Do you see themes across the chapters of your life? Do you see patterns that have defined your behavior today? Do you see beliefs that continually have held you back?

Your most common patterns are likely derived from traits obtained from generational influences, labels placed on you in childhood, and the self-limiting beliefs you developed throughout your life. While some of these rote patterns may have led you to success, they can also block you from your quest for significance. No one winds up living a life of significance while remaining on autopilot. Consider this your exit ramp to shift into a mode of mindfulness as you reflect on life as you know it.

Generational Influences

As children, we internalize or unconsciously assimilate to the environment in which we grew up. Many of us, to differing degrees, have not fully differentiated from our childhood environment, causing us to live our lives from a place of conditioned patterns we absorbed along the way.

Without fail, we all carry within us generational influences. These influences are traits, behaviors, or worldviews that have been passed down from one generation to the next. In some sense, our lives become prescribed by the input from our family of origin and the lens it created for us to see the world.

Parents can be giants in our lives, especially depending on how they parented us. Many of us have parents we admire. They were hard working or honest. They may have taught us the importance of serving the community or helped us cultivate a deep faith in God. Some may have had parents who left us searching for role models outside the home. They may have drank too much or were constantly out of work. They may have been dishonest or negative. And yet for others, their parents lie somewhere in between. They are good yet flawed people making their way through life the best they can.

When clients tell their stories to me, they often tell me they do not want to be like their parents. They hope they are raising their children differently or not focused on work as much. They hope they aren't as negative about the future or always worried about finances. Once we begin to look at the patterns across their own life, we often see that they are navigating their journey much in the same way as those who first influenced them.

The realization that we are more like our parents than we thought can be a shocking discovery for some. Once we outline the characteristics of our parents and grandparents, it doesn't take long to realize that we have spent a good portion of our lives wrestling through the push and pull of these generational patterns within ourselves. We accept and hold up the traits we see as positive—"I inherited my dad's quick wit"—and deny or ignore those we deem as negative—"My mom can be so quick tempered."

In addition to individual traits, it is helpful to list the values or beliefs that were held in high regard by your family as a whole. These values may have had a positive or negative effect on the family dynamic or environment. Did your family value achievement, image, faith, adventure, work, or humor? Did your family have secrets to hide, conflict, addiction, or financial struggles? Were there cultural dynamics that shaped the way you see the world today?

Trauma or the result of trauma can also be behaviorally passed down in families. Much research has been devoted to the many children of abusers who have become abusive in adulthood.[16] Parents can also pass down their pessimistic worldview created by trauma they experienced in their own childhood. For instance, a mother who had been sexually abused as a child may have heightened anxiety around the safety of her young daughter. When the time comes for her child to attend a sleepover or an extended playdate, she may refuse the invitation or allow her to go but then will call her several times to check on her or even pick her up early. Her daughter quickly learns that the world is unsafe and she should be fearful of others. Simply put, anxious parents can create anxious children. You can easily see how a pattern can continue for generations without self-awareness and reframing.

The consequences of our generational influences are profound and can continue to shape our worldview today. We may strive to be generous, successful, creative, loyal, humorous, or honest. We may also come across as secretive, codependent, selfish, emotionally shut down, negative, or angry.

We look at our family of origin not in an effort to place blame on anyone. It is too easy to say it was Mom's or Dad's fault instead of taking responsibility for the behaviors we continue to exhibit today. Rather than shifting the blame, we examine the family structures we came from in order to move into a healthier place of understanding and even redemption.

As we awaken to this different approach of examining ourselves, we break the chains of living a prescribed and conditioned life. This newfound clarity helps us trade in the belief that we are tethered to these generational progressions for the knowledge that there is a way to break our ongoing negative patterns.

We can become the ancestor who changes our bloodline and breaks the generational pattern. We can do the work that those before us either couldn't or wouldn't do.

I witnessed my father pave a new path for his own family. My dad never drank a drop of alcohol when I was growing up. I remember asking him about it when I was a teenager. He told me several stories about his father being an alcoholic, which brought a lot of shame and pain onto his family. My father had vowed to break the line. He was not going to slip into alcoholism and pass it down to his children.

Just like no person is perfect, no family is perfect. That's okay. We are not in search of that Norman Rockwell picture-perfect family. We are instead looking to cherish the good and break the unhelpful patterns as we create a more significant future. Like my dad discovered, it is in finding self-awareness and naming and claiming those traits for our family tree and for ourselves that we begin to experience greater freedom.

Once you follow the root of the pattern, you can then begin to eradicate it by reframing the trait, belief, or behavior. Reframing is breaking the habits that don't serve you well and replacing them with ones that do. People who are successful at this are those who trade one for one.

When you look at your family line, do you recognize any repeated traits or themes? Do you see patterns that have caused pain from one generation to the next?

Labels

Throughout our lives, people can assign labels to us that shape our identities. Some of those labels can be seen as useful, benefiting how we approach our future. Others can be negative or based on stereotypes or minor character traits we exhibited in moments of our lives rather than permanent elements of our personality. Regardless, these labels affect how we see ourselves, how others see us, and, in turn, how we are treated.

Labels are classifying phrases told to us implicitly or explicitly by our family members or authority figures who can shape the narrative of who we are in our mind. You become "the good kid," "the bad kid," "the smart one," "the C student," "the little one," "the chatterbox," "the wallflower" "the pretty one," "the successful one." These labels begin to own us, and they are hard to break after a while. Even when we want to break them, often our family won't let us. I find that I can still feel like I am sixteen years old when I'm around my family. The labels come out, and I shrink. I am fifty years old! How is this possible?

Labels are tough to rewrite. Some we don't want to rewrite. I like being thought of as the overachiever most of the time. Most days it gives me a sense of pride, but some days it's exhausting. Listing our labels gives us power over them.

I find that most of my clients have never seen their labels written down on paper, but the benefits can be groundbreaking. Listing our labels is a powerful process that helps us recognize how they affect our past and are still playing a role in our present. This listing process helps us uncover if these labels are helpful in understanding our personality and behavior, or if they are unhelpful and need to be examined for the detrimental effect they may be having on our view of ourselves.

Once listed, it is also helpful to trace the origin of each label. Positive labels given to us by parents, teachers, mentors, and others can give us confidence to pursue goals. They can give us perseverance and raise our self-esteem. Hearing a teacher tell us we are a talented writer or a relative tell us we have a wonderful singing voice can give us the boost we need to keep cultivating a talent. Oprah Winfrey tells a story about how when she was a child, one of her teachers labeled her as the smart one. "You always have a book in your hand." This sparked in her a lifelong pursuit in learning.

By contrast, seemingly positive or benign labels may lead to suppressing parts of your innate self. For instance, being labeled "the quiet one" or "easygoing" despite having much more to say may lend itself to a long road of suppressing your voice, avoiding conflict, and abandoning your opinion.

You must work to identify all the labels you have been given and dismantle them. Which ones do you want to own, and which ones must be let go of forever?

Self-Limiting Beliefs

No one talks to us more than we talk to ourselves. The constant and continual script playing in our head is incredibly influential and shapes our perspective about ourselves, others, and the world around us. Much of these beliefs and the scripts they create reflect our experiences up to this point. The words or expectations people spoke into our lives, whether good or bad, became our beliefs. Even society—advertisers, movies, celebrities—has shaped how we see ourselves, both internally and externally.

Some beliefs are helpful and keep us from harm. If we cheated in school and were then punished, we come to believe that cheating is wrong. This is a healthy belief that protects us from harm in the future. Our healthy beliefs will serve us well.

But oftentimes there are experiences or people in our lives who have caused us to create self-limiting beliefs. These beliefs are the negative assumptions you hold about yourself and your place in the world. These beliefs rob you of the mental strength you need to grow as a leader, take risks or tackle new opportunities, achieve your goals, or ultimately reach your full potential.

A parent who too often jumped in to solve your problems may have led you to believe you aren't capable enough to resolve issues on your own. A parent who left home never to return may have led you to believe that you aren't genuinely lovable. A grandparent who overpraised you as a child may have left you with a belief that you were being pacified and feedback isn't trustworthy. A teacher who scolded you in front of the class due to a wrong answer may have left you believing you aren't as intelligent as your peers.

One of the most prominent self-limiting beliefs I encounter in my work is imposter syndrome, which is loosely defined as doubting your abilities and feeling like a fraud. It disproportionately affects high-achieving people who find it difficult to accept their accomplishments. Many question whether they deserve accolades. Many executives and leaders still feel, much like I did long ago, as if they are "faking it 'til they make it."

Interestingly, we believe these stories we tell ourselves protect us in some way, but they do quite the opposite. Mark Manson, author of *The Subtle Art of Not Giving A F*ck*, explains,

> We like to imagine ourselves to be the victims of our own limiting beliefs, but the truth is that we adopt these beliefs because they serve us in some way... Generally, we hold onto limiting beliefs for the same reasons—to protect ourselves from struggle and failure. Also, we often hold onto limiting beliefs because they make us feel special, self-righteous or that we deserve special attention.[17]

We have become splintered as individuals. These self-limiting beliefs have made it hard to feel the wholeness of who we are, yet we sit in them because it feels too unsafe or scary to let them go. We have created unhealthy, incorrect identities that eventually lead to self-fulfilling prophecies, causing vicious cycles that keep us stuck in destructive habits.

Seeing we are the ones hanging onto these beliefs, we are the only ones who can debunk them. The best way to stop the cycle is to replace each lie with a liberating truth, but first we must identify them. Many of our beliefs reside in the subconscious, and recognizing the pivot points of our story helps us to do the work of uncovering them. Looking back across each of your pivot points in

Chapter Three, ask yourself, "What did I believe about myself after that happened?"

Recognizing and writing down the repeated scripts in your head is another key exercise in identifying self-limiting beliefs. What are the repeated phrases that plague you most days? What lies do you believe about yourself?

Picking a topic or specific struggle you are currently having and writing the beliefs around that struggle is another way of uncovering the untruths. Maybe you want to start a business or go for a particular promotion at work. Perhaps you are struggling with being confident in front of those you deem superior to you. Name the struggle and then write down the beliefs that come to mind when you think about what is holding you back.

When we sit with those beliefs, we are able to take them out of the darkness and into the light. We are able to expose them for what they are. Moments. Words. Sometimes damaging and oftentimes unfair, but still just moments and still just words.

Once we have uncovered our limiting beliefs, we must rewrite new, truthful beliefs. Rewriting those scripts can be a powerful catalyst for a brighter future. Instead of thinking, *I am not good enough*, I write, *I am still learning and growing and therefore doing the best I can in this moment.* I can replace *I need to make things perfect* with *it's about progress, not perfection.* I replace *I am not a good parent* with *I love my children and am showing up the best I can at this moment.*

Once you have rewritten new truths, you must train your brain to accept them. Your human mind has been conditioned with these limiting beliefs for the majority of your life. It will take some effort to recondition it. You must reread and even meditate on your new truths. There are many techniques on how to do this. You can adopt Transcendental Meditation and spend time each day sitting on a new truth. You can simply reread your key truths each night before bed and each morning at the start of your day. You can print them out and hang them on your bathroom mirror. You can place objects on your desk, like a crystal or stone, to remind you of your new beliefs. Pick it up throughout the day when the old scripts pop into your head. A new, positive mantra can change your mind and ultimately change your life.

Changing your unhealthy beliefs will not happen overnight. Limiting beliefs set up a battle between your true nature and your imagined best self. The longer you carry untruths about yourself in your head, the harder it is to rewrite the script. Nonetheless, the work must be done to unravel and rewrite it, or the second half cannot be better than the first. We have to recognize and break patterns to live fully in our unique talents and live out our mission. Daily renewal of our mind and heart is essential for an intentional life. It is a journey that isn't always easy but is always worth it.

Overcorrection of Patterns

While we're on the subject of patterns passed down to us, for those of us who find ourselves as parents now, it's vital to not overcorrect the course for our children. While most parents today are trying their best, I see several trying a bit too hard. Many of us from Generation

X are products of latchkey parenting. Our parents worked and were rarely present. We all wore a house key around our neck to let us into empty homes, where we were left to fend for ourselves or battle it out with our siblings. This has led to overparenting today. Some parents insist on being *very* present and controlling outcomes. They want their children to have it all, be it all, and do it all.

We are supposed to be preparing our child for the path of life. But today, we spend more time preparing the path, not the child, in an effort to rectify the gaps in our own childhood and making sure the coast is clear for their merit success. Sadly, I've watched children with the brightest of futures either wither under the pressure of their parents' worship or become incapable of navigating the real world on their own.

I conducted an interview with a promising young man straight out of college, whom we'll call Tyler. I could see there were some issues, but I ultimately felt he could be coached and trained. I called to offer Tyler a position as a sales assistant at HGTV. I gave him the details of the position, including salary and benefits. He asked if he could think about it overnight and call back in the morning. I said that would be perfectly fine.

The next morning, Tyler didn't call me, but Tyler's dad did.

He said his son had given him the details of the offer and he was calling to "help him negotiate a salary." He told me what he thought would be a fair salary, after having looked into the market. I said to him, "This is a sales environment where we negotiate multimillion-dollar media deals and train people up to negotiate.

You're not taking this job, your son is." After he debated me on this point of view and gave me additional thoughts on our interviewing process and his opinions on the network, I ended up rescinding the offer. I said, "I'm going to let you be the one to tell Tyler that this position is no longer available to him. If, down the road, he'd like to interview again, on his own, he can."

Tyler's father got very upset with me, as you can imagine. I said, "Look, he's right out of college. I'm hoping this is a turning point for you and him. It's time for him to spread his wings and fly. I can't hire someone knowing that his dad might be on the phone every single time something goes wrong at work, or every time you don't like what he experienced, or a decision I made, or something his teammate did. I can't hire somebody knowing his dad has this much control over his life." It was a clear example of how many parents are overcorrecting, coming from a generation where maybe their parents were less involved and they just had to "be home by dinnertime." It is possible the pendulum has swung too far the other way.

Committing to a life of significance shows your children how to live fully and abundantly without the need for overcorrection. When our children see this in us, they learn to see life as a gift and the world as filled with opportunity. It kicks off a new generation of freedom and discovery but one within a grounded framework of purpose and meaning.

GETTING PAST OUR PAST

> *"It is never too late to be what you might have been."*
>
> —GEORGE ELIOT, *MIDDLEMARCH*

Diving into the past can often feel like opening up Pandora's Box. Do we really want to go there, or is the past better left untouched? Opening up your past has many benefits that are worth the price, but there are some prerequisites to jumping into this process.

First, you must have grace, or true compassion, even if it doesn't seem deserved. Grace for yourself and grace for others that were part of your story up to this point. It is only with a grace perspective that you can recognize, name, forgive, find real truth, and move forward.

A major life shift happens once we stop seeing our parents, relatives, and the other adults who shaped our childhood as giants and more like imperfect people just like us.

On the flipside, some of us may find ourselves fixated on the very worst of our parents, relatives, or teachers and allow those disturbing memories to overshadow the best.

To take a balanced look at our past, we must remember that people are flawed. It is not until we can look at ourselves and others in our life with empathy that we can heal and rewrite our story. When we are able to see humans who did the best they could with what knowledge and ability they had, we are able to let go of blame and face our own responsibility for our current behaviors or beliefs.

That being said, there may be people in our lives who won't let us break the patterns of the past. Part of letting go and moving forward may include making those in our life, especially our family members, aware of the reframing work we are currently doing. This may involve telling them that certain labels hurt, that you are working to break key generational influences, and that you are remedying unhelpful behaviors from your life. Many of your family members may support you or even join your effort to break the patterns of your tribe. Others may not buy into the process and find comfort in keeping things the same. Putting space between you and people who are toxic or harmful, while sad and difficult, is often a necessary step to find complete healing.

Confronting others in our quest to break patterns can be one of the most difficult parts of moving past our past. Regardless, without this type of confrontation, ending behaviors and labels that have held us back will not be possible.

Lastly, embrace your entire past as the foundation for which your life was built—warts and all.

Who you are striving to become is much more important than who you were in the past.

Unfortunately, the person in your past haunts you. You often forget that this person was younger, more naïve, less educated, and more ignorant. But without all that you experienced in your past, you would not have gotten to where you are today. You cannot change your past, but you can change how you view it.

When we can learn to tell our story and also come to appreciate it, we become free to listen and value the stories of others. We discover that people are more than what we see on the surface. This is powerful in helping bridge the great divides of society. As Marjorie Hinckley says, "There isn't a person you wouldn't love if you could read their whole story."

EMBRACING NEW GROWTH

The relationship you have with yourself is the most essential one to invest in. No one can be as intimate and know you as well as you know yourself. Therefore you are the only one who can truly change your life for the better. It takes time to reframe or break the patterns imprinted on us over decades of our life. Awareness is a big game changer, but it is only the beginning. In many ways, we are our minds. The thoughts that inhabit our daily lives control our actions, reactions, decisions, and ultimately our relationships—with others and ourselves. It is not until we can operate with a mature control over our thought life that we can achieve a meaningful impact.

Like pulling weeds in a flower bed, you have to be on your knees, get your hands dirty, and pull up from the root to truly eliminate the toxic shrub. As every gardener knows, if you simply break the weed off at the ground, you risk it sneaking back with even stronger roots. In your own life, you must get to the root of your limiting patterns once and for all so they don't sneak back stronger. After eliminating the weeds, and in preparation for future plant growth, it's time to add a fresh layer of soil. Now that you've eliminated the toxic thoughts and beliefs grounded in the past, and in preparation for your future self-growth, it's time to add a fresh mindset.

Reflections

- As you reflect on your life, past and present, what are the labels, limiting beliefs, and generational influences you see?
- Take some time to cross out the labels you no longer wish to carry, rewrite the limiting beliefs into positive affirmations, and recognize the generational patterns that need to be ended.

CHAPTER FIVE

YOUR MINDSET

"It's not what you look at that matters; it's what you see."

—HENRY DAVID THOREAU

In 2021, Jeff Bezos's privately funded company Blue Origin began launching rockets to the edge of space with civilian passengers. It was exciting to see William Shatner become a real-life version of Captain Kirk, going where no (regular) man has gone before!

After being flung so far away, Shatner described the experience as both moving and unbelievable. "I hope I never recover from this. I hope that I can maintain what I feel now," he said upon returning back to Earth. "I don't want to lose it."

The ability to get above it all and see what is truly big and truly small creates a powerful new shift in awareness. Similarly, the process of creating a Strategic Life Map for your journey ahead requires a powerful new shift in awareness—a new mindset.

In the previous chapters you had an opportunity to go deep within your own story and zoom out for a 360-degree view of your world. By examining your story, you've also uncovered patterns that could continue to weigh you down and fog up the windshield.

If you genuinely want to live out your purpose and realize the life you want, you must replace your old way of looking at things. It's time to put on a new pair of glasses and kick on the defogger. Instead of seeing your patterns as problems, I want you to see them as your personal invitation to adopt a new mindset.

ONE GIANT LEAP OF FAITH

It's a huge leap of faith to board one of these Blue Origin rockets. Before launch, there is a window of two minutes and thirty seconds where passengers can back out of the flight with a simple phrase: "I will not fly." I can only imagine that those two minutes and thirty seconds are some of the longest moments of their lives.

When I decided to resign from HGTV, I had to call our chief revenue officer to share my decision. It was not just a formality for me. Over the many years we had worked together, he had been an important mentor and advocate for my career. He was not thrilled with my decision and told me he was unwilling to accept my resignation without me sleeping on it one more night. Then he hung up the phone.

I sat at my desk in a moment of disbelief. Was my time at HGTV finished or not? Even though I had spent roughly two years weighing the pros and cons of this enormous decision, I went home to ruminate one more night.

Would I opt out, or would I fly?

I would certainly fly.

Leaving HGTV felt a bit like leaving the only planet I had really known in my adulthood. I was taking off for what felt like another universe. Once I accepted my mission to explore a new frontier, my view on life was never the same. Leaving a place of relative comfort and acceptance for a new adventure opened my eyes in ways I could have never imagined.

Are you ready to open your eyes? Are you ready to fly? Think of this point in the book as your opt-out window. If you do not feel like you are ready to adopt an expanded way of thinking and viewing your world, then it might be time to tap out of this process.

But if you find yourself ready to evolve toward a larger perspective on your life, then it's time to adopt the right mindset to shape, sharpen, and support the work ahead and create the life you want.

THE GREAT MIND SHIFT

> *"The significant problems we face cannot be solved at the same level of thinking we were at when we created them."*
>
> —ALBERT EINSTEIN

One of the problems with midlife is we can become set in our ways. After so many years of conditioning, we tend to see the world not as *it is* but as *we are*. Established perspectives are hard to crack. Pushing past what we believe to be true in hopes of seeing a bigger picture doesn't come naturally for most.

Radical, lasting change does not happen by altering our external situations. It occurs only when we encounter true self-awareness and shift first from within.

Cognitive neuroscientist and author of *Switch On Your Brain*, Dr. Caroline Leaf, points out that we often conflate the mind and the brain, but they are two different things. The brain is a physical organ, made up of cells, keeping the body functioning and you alive. The mind is an infinite force that goes beyond the brain; it is an energy field giving us the ability to think, choose, and feel. The mind is the force that pushes through, directs, and causes growth of the brain.

As Dr. Leaf puts it, "Your body is not in control of your mind—your mind is in control of your body, and your mind is stronger than your body. Mind certainly is over matter."[18]

Changing our mind—or instead making the choice to change specific mindsets in our life—can change our brain, body, and spirit. Anxiety, stress, toxic thinking, and negative thought patterns must be managed through our mind to live a life of purpose and intention. Your mind can and will hold you back if you don't manage it.

If you want to change the direction you are headed, you must first change your mind. People tend to lean on self-help techniques to change their behavior or attitude in hopes of bettering themselves and their lives. We think a "new and improved," disciplined version of ourselves will solve our dissatisfaction and lead us in a better direction. But trying on a new habit in hopes of permanent change will not help us determine our next, best step in life. Like a fad diet, it is hard to maintain if it is based on a quick-fix mentality. We must go deeper. We are looking for a complete lifestyle change, which will take a great mind shift.

As Dr. Leaf says, "We can manage our minds. Our minds are malleable. It's a skill that we can actually learn. It's not a therapy technique. It's not a little magic trick. This is hardcore science."

Examining how we got to where we are today exposed the depth and sources of our negative patterns. Now it is time to ensure that our roots are healthy and in fertile soil. Turns out that fertile soil can only be cultivated with healthy perspectives and proper mindsets.

THREE SIGNIFICANT MINDSETS

> *"Don't live the same year 75 times and call it a life."*
>
> **—ROBIN SHARMA**

We can count on life to bring us what we need in order to grow in the right direction. The hard part is being awake enough to embrace the learning experience before us.

When I was in college, my dad gave me a book that greatly influenced him called *The Power of Positive Thinking* by Norman Vincent Peale. I remember diving into it on my way back to campus.

It was the first time I was introduced to the power of flushing out "old, tired worn out thoughts" and reframing your perspective. Peale wrote, "As you think, so shall you be." It was as if I was given new empowering lenses through which to see the world.

Perspective is everything. Your perspective will dictate your life trajectory. Several key mindsets are helpful for a life of significance, but the ones I find to be essential are a longevity mindset, a wisdom mindset, and a contentment mindset.

A longevity mindset focuses on believing you will live a long and healthy life. Not believing you have a long road ahead of you means you may shut down long before your time is up. A longevity mindset permanently benefits how you live, think, and act and avoids wasting precious time to make an impactful difference to the world around you.

A wisdom mindset encourages you to embrace a spirit of curiosity and lifelong learning. While most people understand the importance of knowledge, how to obtain true wisdom may be somewhat elusive, and many miss the opportunity to receive more insight into the world around them. But without a wisdom mindset, you may not have the open and accepting mind needed to live out your purpose in an engaging way.

The contentment mindset reminds you to embrace the goodness and grace around you. A life of significance is not an endless pursuit of happiness. Instead, it is a commitment to a satisfying and fulfilling life, no matter the unexpected or the unwelcomed that show up along the way.

Let's look at each one of these mindsets more deeply in hopes of embedding them permanently into our daily lives.

A LONGEVITY MINDSET

"A light heart lives long."

—WILLIAM SHAKESPEARE

I recently turned fifty. The years have passed quickly, but I embraced this milestone birthday with excitement. I was healthy, happy, and feeling strong. All was well until I received my AARP envelope in the mail. AARP stands for the American Association of Retired Persons. Did I miss the memo that I was now at retirement age? The very same month, to add insult to injury, my seventy-six-year-old mother informed me that she was moving into a fifty-five-and-older community. I went to visit her shortly after her move and, despite the description, found that no one under the age of seventy lived in her building.

This led me to wonder—am I out of touch with the reality of my age, or are there some pretty archaic constructs still existing in our society?

As someone who has been in television for decades, I thought I'd turn to television for a reality check. The stark difference in approach to television sitcoms today from when I was growing up in the 1970s is palpable. Today the characters in midlife are portrayed as more energetic and connected. For example, Claire and Phil Dunphy of today's popular sitcom *Modern Family* are in their forties. Archie and Edith Bunker of the hit 1970s sitcom *All in the Family* were also in their mid-forties yet looked elderly by comparison.

The actresses staring in the late 1980s popular sitcom *The Golden Girls* were all in their fifties—the same ages of the actresses starring in the *Sex and the City* reboot, *And Just Like That*. I think it is fair to say that there is a vast difference not only in the look but also the lifestyle of these two sets of friends.

The Quest for Rest

Indeed, today's television landscape has changed. I believe it reflects how our society is not only physically reversing the signs of aging but also mentally relating to retirement.

The retirement age has really blurred when you consider another hit sitcom today, *Grace & Frankie*. It stars Jane Fonda, who has always been devoted to her physical and mental health; she looks amazing at her age. But it is more than just her outward beauty that piques my interest. She is still engaged and working well into her eighties. Alongside her costars, Lily Tomlin, Martin Sheen, and Sam Waterston, also in their eighties, Fonda shows up each day delivering lines and seemingly having a blast.

In her TED Talk, Fonda talks about what she calls "The Third Act." She notes how we are living approximately thirty-four years longer than our great-grandparents. She asks, "What are you going to do with your extra thirty years?" She points out that feeling young is a *feeling* inside your head. You tell your brain how old you are.

> The old paradigm was: You're born, you peak at midlife, and then you decline into decrepitude. Looking at aging as ascending a staircase, you gain well-being, spirit, soul, wisdom, the ability to be truly intimate and a life with intention. This optimistic perspective honors the aging process.

Our television families are not the only thing that is aging differently. Terminology is also evolving. I hardly hear people use the word *retirement*. It is as though the word itself has retired. People now talk about their "last act" or what they'll do once they leave the work world or live life on their own terms.

In a recent *Wall Street Journal* article, author John Stoll investigated "The End of Retirement." He interviewed economist Olivia Mitchell, a professor at the University of Pennsylvania's Wharton School of Business, who stated,

> When people leave school, it's not going to be for twenty- or thirty-year careers, it's going to be for a fifty-year career... Actuaries (the people trying to figure out how long beneficiaries will live), are now projecting people entering the workforce could live 125 years. And that's just a starting point... Some demographers say the baby who will live to 200 years old is already born. People in their sixties today look very much like people in their forties not long ago.[19]

The need for a plan to take you into the second half of your life is greater than it has ever been before. Those who have an idea of where to go next and how to best invest their future are those reaping the biggest benefit from our newly extended life spans.

Longevity Mindset Defined

Instead of planning for the end of life, we can and should plan for a longer life. Instead of winding down around the traditional retirement age, we can embrace a new phase of living life with vigor and engagement. We see many more exciting chapters ahead!

This takes a longevity mindset. A longevity mindset is when you choose to wholeheartedly believe that a long and healthy life is normal and attainable. You believe that aging can be managed rather than accepted as a limiting fate.

When embracing a longevity mindset, it is important to understand the difference between life expectancy and life span. A life span refers to the maximum number of years a person *can* live, while life expectancy refers to a statistical measure of the average number of years a person can *expect* to live. It is a prediction. While there are a lot of factors that appear outside of our direct control, such as health issues, life circumstances, genetics, and the unexpected, a longevity mindset simply rejects this number. It rejects the social norm that nothing can be done about it. Research shows that our lifestyle choices and our mindset are the true driving forces of the years that await us. This means that much of our life expectancy rests in our own hands.

A longevity mindset means letting go of predetermined life expectancy averages and embracing a life span well beyond the societal norm. Rather than lamenting the years that have passed, you name the age you *want* to live until and consciously live with the belief that you have that number of years ahead of you. Your mind has the power to positively affect your life span. Use that power.

A longevity mindset provides an opportunity to replace the long, hard-wired belief that traditional retirement is inevitable. If you still need some convincing, consider waking up to the fact that retirement isn't as good for your health as you might think. While parts of retirement can bring much needed rest and relaxation, research shows a strong correlation between early retirement and mortality. One study found that people who retire at fifty-five are 89 percent more likely to die within ten years than those who retire at sixty-five.[20] Another study found that men who retire at sixty-two have a 20 percent higher likelihood of death than the general population.

My brother-in-law in Ireland comes from a hardworking farming family. For generations his family has worked the land on the top of a mountain in the rural countryside of county Kerry. Over the course of several years, he and his siblings lovingly encouraged their dad to retire so he could enjoy life and finally relax. Their father protested, saying he didn't want to relax and believed he'd be dead within a year if he didn't keep busy with his work. He finally gave in and retired. Nine months later, he passed away suddenly and unexpectedly. While this story is anecdotal, it led me to consider whether completely disconnecting from our professions has to feel like a mandatory step in the aging process.

A longevity mindset doesn't mean we need to work for the rest of our lives, but when we lean into the work that fulfills us and gives us opportunities to live our purpose, it can be life-giving rather than life-taking. We may choose to work fewer hours than we did in our twenties, having new agency over our lives that years of experience affords us. This new way of working can renew our perspective on the idea of having a vocation into our older years.

Perceiving that life is over at fifty or believing it's all downhill from here can become a self-fulfilling prophecy that must be avoided. Framing our life as a hill to climb in order to reach a pinnacle sets us up for resignation and disappointment, because it means that everything else is downhill or declining. We will prove ourselves right about whatever we believe, so why not believe the best is yet to come?

Achieving a Longevity Mindset

Here are a few ways to take initiative and ensure that your longevity mindset sticks.

Be Social: Research shows that those who believe they are going to die at the commonly dictated age of seventy-five will begin to wind down socially roughly ten years earlier. Slowing down to some can mean more time in front of our devices and less time planning social activities. This can lead to boredom or loneliness. Who wants to live longer if they find life boring or lonely? Those with a longevity mindset lean into life. They join social activities like exercise classes, walking groups, dinner parties, and group travel experiences. Meeting new people not only grows our minds but breathes excitement into life.

Connect with Those Younger Than You: Younger friends will keep you savvy to what is important to the up-and-coming generations. They bring fresh perspectives and, most importantly, fresh energy to your life. Many younger people are looking for mentorship and guidance. These opportunities give us purpose and meaning.

Embrace Your Medical Journey: You won't be successful in living longer and healthier if you aren't connected to the right medical professionals. Simply screening annually for common diseases, while essential, isn't enough. The goal is to not just stay alive but to thrive. Find doctors who believe in mixing Western and Eastern medicine and challenge themselves to stay abreast of the latest medical advances. Stop investing your time, money, and energy in doctors who do not care or are uninterested in your longevity mission. Make appointments well in advance for all areas of your health. Listen to health podcasts; read books by cutting edge, qualified doctors and scientists; and join longevity-minded groups to expand your education on health and wellness initiatives.

Enlist Others to Join You: Having a longevity mindset will be hard to maintain on your own. Tell your spouse, family, and closest friends about your decision to accept a longevity mindset. Tell them you want your long and healthy life to include them. Ask them to name the age they want to live until and then invite them along on your educational journey.

A longevity mindset is key to a life of significance. When we believe wholeheartedly that we have decades ahead of us, we lean into life! We learn more and love more. A longevity mindset fills us with the energy and optimism we need to live the life we want.

A WISDOM MINDSET

> *"Yesterday I was clever, so I wanted to change the world. Today I am wise, so I want to change myself."*
>
> —RUMI

In many popular books and movies, the wise character is apparent: Yoda, Dumbledore, Mr. Miyagi, Mary Poppins. They are the protagonists' mentor, teacher, and guide.

One of my favorite wise characters is Gandalf from the popular *Lord of the Rings* trilogy. While he is a man who has the power of a wizard, it is his thoughtful and patient presence that makes him a wise mentor to the various hero characters of the stories. He sometimes leans in with words of wisdom or encouragement. He sometimes keeps quiet to give space for the growth and development of those he cares most about. But he can also be bold and a seemingly fearless fighter against the evil tyranny of the antagonists.

The Lord of the Rings is riddled with examples of characters wrestling with their purpose and place in the world. Many characters are forced to either embrace their purpose or try to escape it. Gandalf serves as a wise counselor to many as they wrestle with choosing the right path. His most important influence is over one key hero, a hobbit named Frodo.

In one deeply meaningful scene in the first book, there is an exchange between the two characters.

I wish it need not have happened in my time," said Frodo. "So do I," said Gandalf, "and so do all who live to see such times. But that is not for them to decide. All we have to decide is what to do with the time that is given us.[21]

Frodo has learned the destructive nature of the infamous ring and what it will mean for his world. Gandalf's words to Frodo are filled with wisdom. First, he affirms Frodo. He agrees that it is hard. Then he encourages and guides. He tells Frodo that we must rise to the challenge given each of us. We must face the suffering rather than escape it. But he goes further. Gandalf suggests that we have been born during a certain time, for a reason, and there is a purpose that each of us is meant to fulfill during that time.

Gandalf is deemed wise not because of his intelligence but because he sees the bigger picture. We know he has lived by his long gray hair and tall walking stick. But it is his words and actions that show he has learned, through his many years, the deep truths of his world.

The Quest for Truth

Adam Grant, in his groundbreaking book *Think Again*, says that we tend to cling to three key tools—assumptions, instincts, and habits. We too often forget the tool of having an open mind. [22]

Grant writes, "If knowledge is power, knowing what we don't know is wisdom." We should "favor humility over pride, doubt over certainty, curiosity over closure." With middle age comes the danger of resting too comfortably in our assumptions. It can be easy to stay comfortable in the beliefs and thoughts which make us feel safe or right, even if our information is wrong! Pride and fear breed conviction rather than curiosity.

We need to learn to rethink or, as Grant reminds us, to "think again" if we want to grow in wisdom. As the saying goes, the older you get, the wiser you become. But that is only true if we consciously embrace the quest for what is true.

To be wise we must be more curious than certain. A preschool child asks on average one hundred questions a day. As we age that number drops dramatically. As we approach our middle-aged years, we find it much more comfortable to be the expert than the student. But being the student is key to a wisdom mindset. Those who approach situations with space for questions rather than instant answers are the ones who grow in wisdom.

It takes humility to question your current understanding and push for any information you may be missing. As French writer and moralist Joseph Joubert states, "It is better to debate a question without settling it than to settle a question without debating it." We must not fear that debate but welcome it. While a wise person may seem as though they are the professor, it is their constant curious nature that has provided them with proper perspective.

Wise people diligently and consistently chase after the absolute truth. They embrace what is right even if it feels uncomfortable, and even if it doesn't align with the beliefs of a preferred tribe. This is one reason why wisdom is so rare. Many people would rather hold on to what is most comfortable than what is most true.

But wise people know that comfort can limit and isolate, while wisdom can free us and illuminate the path.

Wisdom Mindset Defined

A wisdom mindset is a belief that as you grow in experience, sound judgment, and compassion, the intuition you develop is more powerful than intelligence alone. It's a belief that you must rest your ego to further your purpose. It is the recognition of the importance of character, values, humility, and truth.

Anybody who wants to grow in knowledge can, but not everyone knows how to root themselves in wisdom. Wisdom is not education. It is not being smart. It is not IQ. Wisdom is not the same as moral goodness. All those things are great to have, especially if you want success, but a life of significance is different.

Wisdom isn't rooted in having a technique but in having character. Wise people are those who have lived experience and have grown from that experience in a way that directs their life and helps them direct others. It is having competence when wrestling with the complex realities of life. It is insight into knowing how things truly work and then an intuitive knowing for what to do about it. It goes beyond "just do it" to "do the right thing." Making the right decisions takes wisdom. Avoiding disaster takes wisdom. Wisdom is the secret ingredient for taking a life of significance from a nice idea to a way of life.

Achieving a Wisdom Mindset

Embracing a wisdom mindset is a growth journey. Here are a few ways to achieve a wisdom mindset.

Have Mentors: I have always been drawn to finding wise mentors in my life. I believe the drive to learn from those who have gone before is one of, if not the single-most, important factors to my success in life. You must be open to and even seek feedback, even if it is uncomfortable. Good mentors are invested in your growth. They are not just there to encourage you but to teach you.

Seek Truth: Let go of the temptation to live in self-imposed ignorance in an effort to stay comfortable or true to toxic tribal beliefs. Do not rest until you know you have established the truth. Study all sides of an argument before landing on where you stand. A wise person can calmly recount the alternative side of a belief. A wise person isn't scared to test or push the boundaries of their opinions. They welcome it as a way to get closer to the absolute truth.

Create a Diverse Friend Group: If your friend group looks and thinks exactly like you then it is time for a change. A wise person surrounds themselves with diversity. They seek out people who are from different races, socioeconomic backgrounds, or different cultural backgrounds. Diverse friends increase our empathy and expand our view of the world. Wise people know that all humans have a story to tell, lessons to teach, and wisdom to share.

Increase Your Emotional Intelligence: I tell all those I coach that the gap between being a good leader and a great one is emotional intelligence (EQ). EQ is your ability to recognize and manage your own emotions as well as those around you. A person with high EQ can name what they are feeling and why. They can self-regulate. They are also able to read a room. They can articulate the environment and manage the situation. EQ is flexible. You can grow your EQ through self-awareness and coaching. Find an EQ coach who can assess and coach you to a higher EQ.

Maintaining a wisdom mindset isn't simply one of personal growth. It is a quest to understand and connect to life as a thoughtful observer. People who are wise understand there is no end to their growth and embrace it.

A CONTENTMENT MINDSET

> *"All his life has he looked away to the future, to the horizon. Never his mind on where he was."*
>
> —YODA

Conor Pass is the highest mountain pass in Ireland. At the top is one of the most beautiful views of the Irish countryside, which might be why it's where my husband chose to ask me to marry him.

It also has one of the most dangerous roads I have ever been on. It's one precarious turn after another on a small road located precariously close to the edge of the mountain. To say it is a struggle to reach the top is an understatement.

Both rich in beauty and ripe for adventure, I think of this stretch of road as a keen metaphor for life. You know that Conor Pass is a hard drive, so you pay attention with heightened awareness. If you don't, you won't make it. You will either fall off the road or give in to the fear and turn back in search of an easier, happier life.

When we wrongly believe that life should be a constant source of happiness, we are sorely disappointed and even shocked when struggles arise. Not only that, but we start to treasure ease and comfort above all else, which leads to unrealistic or even limited expectations.

The Quest for Happiness

If you enter the word happiness while searching for books on Amazon.com, you are served over 50,000 results. It is clear that the quest for happiness is a popular one. Unfortunately, it seems elusive and hard to maintain. Why has no one seemed to be able to solve the happiness problem?

We tend to look at a happy life as binary. We either have it or we do not. This puts pressure on us to feel happy all the time. It is not natural or beneficial. Happiness is often circumstantial. It is based on external factors, which guide us to seek satisfaction from the outside world. When we look to our external environment to satisfy us, then suddenly we are grasping at things we cannot control. This perspective leaves us in a constant state of wanting more. We set ourselves up to compete, compare, or collect. It is an endless pursuit that leaves us empty and frustrated.

At its core, the quest for happiness becomes a quest for more. And as author Glennon Doyle puts it, "We can never have enough of what we don't need."[23]

As you climb the corporate ladder, you get promotions and raises. Soon the things we owned previously seem worn or dated, and we suddenly rationalize an upgrade. Little by little we find a way to spend the new, extra income. These microscopic decisions add up, one after another, and it doesn't take long until we have accumulated a lot. But we often don't see it. Why? Because even rich people don't really see themselves as rich. Unless you are Oprah Winfrey or Bill Gates, most likely you know someone with more money. We all rub elbows with people who make more than we do, and this adds to blindness and lack of contentment.

Where we spend our money and how much we think about money is a clue to how much control money has over our lives.

> ***Follow the money in your life, and you'll get a map of where you believe happiness resides.***

We must pause and think about the hold our money has not only on our lives but on our dreams. If we never have enough, we will not pursue anything that may jeopardize that comfort.

Money often blinds us to the type of career we choose. I find that many people have chosen a job out of college or a career path that will give them the most security or wealth. When they find, several years in, that it is not what they expected or they don't like it, they can't change. The golden handcuffs are snug-fitting, and we are too blind to find the key.

The number one reason people do not live out their true purpose is fear of not making enough money. I coach many CEOs and leaders who have convinced themselves that the only way out is more money. They wish someone would buy their company or they could create a product that makes them rich so they can take off the handcuffs.

You will not be able to make a major life change without remapping your mindset. You must let go of the earthly belongings that control you and hold tighter to the assets that cannot be lost or taken from you.

American author David Foster Wallace gave a now famous commencement address to Kenyon College, where he said this:

> If you worship money and things, if they are where you tap real meaning in life, then you will never have enough, never feel you have enough. It's the truth. Worship your body and beauty and sexual allure and you will always feel ugly. And when time and age start showing, you will die a million deaths before they finally grieve you. On one level, we all know this stuff already. It's been codified as myths, proverbs, clichés, epigrams, parables; the skeleton of every great story. The whole trick is keeping the truth up front in daily consciousness.[24]

It appears that the more people try to create their heaven on earth, the less able they are to enjoy it. As Socrates once said, "Contentment is natural wealth; luxury is artificial happiness." As Wallace said, we must keep this knowledge up front in our consciousness. But this can feel like no easy feat. We know it wasn't for Wallace, who after a long battle with depression ended his life.

I spoke with behavioral scientist, researcher, and author of *The*

Loneliness Epidemic, Susan Mettes, and she puts it this way: "Happiness feels good moment by moment. And then you look back on your life and you're actually not happy about it. You must reframe it around what makes my life satisfying, what makes it worthwhile? What kind of life will I be glad I've lived? And when you start asking those questions, you're able to incorporate some hardship and some suffering and some self sacrifice."

So maybe we are asking ourselves the wrong question. Instead of asking, "How can I be happy?" we need to ask ourselves, "How can I be satisfied?" We must look within rather than outside of ourselves to answer this question. The answer holds the key to our contentment.

It wasn't until I left the nonstop corporate world that I realized how splintered my life had become. I had been pulled in too many directions, and as a side effect, the people I loved were being pulled, too. My life was busy. It was a life of quantity, but my greatest moments of joy were in the moments of quality. Turns out busyness doesn't always equal productivity and fulfillment.

A contentment mindset helped me shift my perspective from the pursuit of productivity and happiness to that of peace and acceptance, regardless of what life would throw my way.

Contentment Mindset Defined

A contentment mindset is the belief that you have enough. It means you consistently accept that in the present moment of your life everything is as it should be, regardless of what you are experiencing. It is the most complete and lasting feeling of well-being.

A contentment mindset is one that is firmly rooted in seeing the abundance of life. It is the belief that there is enough for everyone and therefore there is no need to see life as a continual race or competition to be won.

Contentment comes from the Latin word *contentus*, which means intact or whole. It has evolved over time to mean someone who feels complete or whole. Someone who desires nothing more beyond themselves. A contentment mindset is one that embraces feeling complete.

Because a contentment mindset is based on what you define as a satisfying life, it is based on your life as a whole, not just one factor, role, or experience. This leaves room for us to accept both the highs and the lows, seeing both as necessary for an impactful and meaningful life.

Over the years, I have coached, led, and guided hundreds of people from different walks of life with different worldviews. There have been some who were always angry, struggling, complaining, or in some sort of peril. I have counseled, coached, and even prayed for them, but they never seemed to be able to accept life's burdens, push through them, and rise above. Instead, they looked to blame others and oftentimes even shifted the blame to God. Though they yearn for things to be different, they are stuck. They are the *victims*.

But there have also been those whom I call *joy radiators*. I have watched them laugh and cry. They too have had burdens and trials, but they have an ability to put them into perspective. Rather than feeling like a victim, they weigh hardships against the whole of their lives. They have the unique ability to sit squarely in gratitude and empathy. They may wish to solve their problems, but their pursuit is not of more. They have a contentment mindset.

Contentment beyond our circumstances can best be illustrated by the extraordinary stories of Holocaust survivors, such as Eddie Jaku.

In 1938 Eddie Jaku was taken from his home and spent over seven years in a concentration camp. Eddie faced unimaginable horrors every day, first in Buchenwald, then in Auschwitz, and then on a Nazi death march. He lost family, friends, and his country.

Because he survived, Eddie made a vow to smile every day. He pays tribute to those who were lost by telling his story, sharing his wisdom, and living his best possible life. He now believes he is the happiest man on earth. But he defines happiness not based on more but based on meaning. His happiness is not circumstantial but a sustaining joy.

> Happiness does not fall from the sky; it is in your hands. Happiness comes from inside yourself and from the people you love. And if you are healthy and happy you are a millionaire. And happiness is the only thing in the world that doubles each time you share it. Through all of my years I have learned this: life is beautiful if you make it beautiful.[25]

Eddie did not get to this place overnight. It has been a journey for him. A contentment mindset is a choice that we must make each day upon waking. You may experience the worst on some days and the best on others, but when you choose to maintain the perspective to look at your life in its entirety, you begin to recognize all that is beautiful, the sweetness and the pain, and you're able to rest in the joy of a contented heart.

Achieving a Contentment Mindset

Cultivating a contentment mindset is a daily renewal of your heart and mind. Here are a few ways to practice contentment and create a permanent mindset.

Take Stock Daily: Ask yourself each day, how whole do I feel inside? Because contentment is based on a strong internal centering, not external circumstance, your first step each day should be a focused time of self-awareness. Remind yourself of your talents, giftings, values, and purpose. When you rest more fully in who you are, then you are less dependent on the ever-changing circumstances swirling around you.

Incorporate Gratitude in Your Life: Practicing gratitude is a popular and powerful way to increase contentment in your life. Create or buy a gratitude journal and use it at either the beginning or end of each day. Research shows that doing this activity at the same time each day is most effective. Furthermore, quickly listing five things you feel grateful for has the power to alter your mind. The items that make your list do not have to be big. Sometimes remembering the simple gifts in our lives has the most impact.

Be Generous: When we are generous with our time and money, it exposes us to the power of an abundance mentality. Most people don't give because they are fearful. They tend to think they don't have enough. But small steps of generosity are known to give back a huge sense of satisfaction and contentment. Elizabeth Dunn, a social psychologist at the University of British Columbia and author of *Happy Money: The Science of Happier Spending,* explains that her research shows that it isn't just giving that gives an emotional boost; it is knowing you have had a specific impact. When we see how our money and time affect the lives of others, we feel a sense of purpose and greater contentment.

Creating a contentment mindset may be the hardest challenge of all. We live in a world that is filled with messages and pictures, coaxing us to believe what we have is never enough. There is always something else to buy, someone else to look like, and something else to obtain. Contentment is a daily commitment, but the joy and peace it can bring will unlock the door to a life of significance.

CARPE DIEM NO MORE

"Live each day as if it is your last" is a saying that became very popular when I was in college. I think the charge *carpe diem* was launched into the spotlight by Robin Williams's brilliant portrayal of an English teacher in the 1989 movie *Dead Poets Society*. Like the rest of America, I embraced the philosophy. Unfortunately for me and many others, it got twisted into a panicked hustle mentality. It is a saying that puts the utmost pressure on the agenda of the day, adding to our overall confusion or dissatisfaction. *I have to do it all and as soon as possible, as today may be my last.* It has set us up to rest in a scarcity mentality rather than one of abundance.

Instead, a better way of living may be to understand that we only die once but we have many days to live. Each of those days should be lived fully and intentionally in the present.

The power of longevity, wisdom, and contentment mindsets is that they end up supporting one another. If you genuinely believe you will live into your hundreds, then you look to grow and learn. That curiosity gives way to wisdom and a feeling of abundance, which leads to contentment. And when you're content, why wouldn't you want to live as long as possible?

As Julia Hawkins approached her one-hundredth birthday, her daughter suggested that she sign up to run the one-hundred-meter race. She suggested that her mother attempt to run it in under one hundred seconds. Intrigued by the challenge, Julia trained for the race and ran it in fifty-six seconds. When interviewed for the upcoming Senior Olympics, Julia was asked how she felt about the competition. She responded that the other older runners were just there for fun but she was an athlete.

Bestselling author James Clear writes in his book *Atomic Habits*, "Don't just read a book or have a reading routine; become a reader. Don't just run a marathon or work out regularly; become a runner. To fulfill your potential, keep expanding and elevating your identity." [26]

You will stick with your Life Vision when it becomes part of who you are rather than just a goal you have set for yourself. When it becomes your lifestyle, it becomes your mindset.

With your mind properly positioned, you are ready to move forward and dig deeper into your life-mapping process. It is time to discover with a new set of eyes who you are and why you exist. It is time to craft a compass that will guide you through the next chapters of your life.

Reflections

- How would you rate your view of, and commitment to, a Longevity, Wisdom, and Contentment Mindset?
- How can you best optimize each of these Mindsets in your life?

PART TWO

WHY DO I EXIST?

There is no passion to be found playing small—
in settling for a life that is less than the
one you are capable of living.

—NELSON MANDELA

CHAPTER SIX

YOUR LIFE COMPASS

"The two most important days of your life are the day you are born and the day you find out why."

—MARK TWAIN

Did you ever see Julia Roberts and Richard Gere in *Runaway Bride*? It's not quite the *Pretty Woman* I had been hoping for, but it does paint a picture of how discovering our true unique selves isn't always a piece of cake.

The story goes that Julia's character, Maggie, a woman who has been engaged three times, has left all her fiancés at the altar and is hoping that the fourth time's a charm. Richard Gere's character,

Ike, a reporter from New York City, comes along with his big city attitude, not buying Maggie's Julia-ness (cue occasional Southern accent), and starts to dissect her behavior. In one pivotal scene, it all comes down to eggs.

Maggie likes different styles of eggs because she's constantly shifting her preferences to what her *fiancé du jour* wants her to like.

Ike: "You were so lost you didn't even know what kind of eggs you liked! With the priest, you wanted scrambled. With the deadhead, it was fried..."

Maggie: "That is called changing your mind."

Ike: "No, that's called not having a mind of your own."

Maggie is a character riddled with insecurity and codependence due to an uncertainty of who she really is and what she really wants.

Just like when Ike challenged Maggie on how she prefers her eggs, and more deeply, who she uniquely is and what she desires, there are moments in all of our lives that bring us to a standstill.

For me, it was my RA diagnosis and the physical pain that brought me to a standstill and provided an early invitation to an essential awakening. Through grief and discomfort, I began a journey I continue to be on today to find connection to the innate parts of me that had been lying dormant. It was as if my broken body was reintroducing me to my sleepy mind and soul—both eager to reemerge and connect to a higher, more alive version of myself. In a new sense, it was time to grow again. Saying goodbye to the younger, more naïve girl, including the influences, labels, and limiting beliefs that no longer served me.

Spoiler alert: this process didn't happen overnight. There was a large part of me obscured by an imagined self. That person was seemingly thriving and surviving, but it wasn't entirely truthful or comfortable. Over time, there was a wrestling developing within me that was beginning to surface.

It would be another decade before I allowed myself the luxury to fully indulge in a process to actually go there. The imagined self was successful and on a trajectory, after all. I had some expectations to fulfill. A marriage and a promotion on the horizon. A television network to help lead and children to have. Understanding the complexity of that inner struggle takes a certain maturity and amount of space that I had yet to realize. But I'd get there eventually, and it was in my forties when I finally confronted the struggle within. It was then I allowed myself to find out what kind of eggs I liked.

WHO ARE YOU?

After reflecting on our past and better understanding who we are not, we are often left with one big question—who am I, really? This is a healthy and helpful question that shouldn't be avoided. But answering it can sometimes feel like a moving target.

Maybe the pressure to answer such a big question seems too elusive and impractical. To some it can even seem silly and pointless. So we avoid it altogether.

But it is in the answer that we can find true clarity in living our lives rather than just enduring them. It is when we identify our identity that we come to admire ourselves in a new way and lead our lives with greater impact. The answer takes us off the conveyor belt of working until the next vacation and puts us on a journey to a fulfilling and meaningful existence.

Rather than derailing ourselves by turning it into some endless pilgrimage, let's simplify it.

Answering the right questions to unlock who you genuinely are will give you a compass that correctly guides you on your journey.

Your Life Compass Questions:

- What are you best at?
- What do you care about?
- How do you want to behave?
- Why do you exist?

Your Life Compass is comprised of your unique talents, the current passions of your heart, your personal core values, and your core purpose. When you understand and articulate these four key components, they will shape and guide the goals you lay out for your years ahead.

We build significant companies answering these questions, and we can do the same with our lives. In business, it is a given that we strategize to articulate a mission statement, craft a vision, and define core values for our company. We inspire and empower our employees by reminding them why the company exists and how they can contribute to the greater purpose of the business. Through these much-accepted practices, our teams gain the clarity needed to operate efficiently and effectively. Many attribute their success and profits to the unwavering commitment to their carefully crafted mission statement along with the vision and values that drive it.

What if we could accomplish the same for our lives? What if our defined talents, core values, and passions gave us the purpose we needed to reach the goal of a meaningful and significant life?

The personal benefits to us are great. Our Life Compass keeps us from feeling lost or hopeless. It keeps us on course. It guides us toward connections to society and to others, which keeps us from feeling alienated or isolated. Having clear direction, much like with a company, can also give you more economic stability. Knowing what we are good at and how to use those talents in a way that is most fulfilling to us can enable us to find the right job, stay in it longer, and be more successful at it.

No matter what stage of life you are in, creating a Life Compass for yourself can serve as a filter for your decisions and provide peace to a restless heart.

You Are Not Your Work

Before we dive deeper into crafting a Life Compass, it's important to get out of the false identity trap set by the roles in our lives. Identity is a tricky word in a world of curated selves. It's harder than ever to find who we truly are under the pile of Instagram pictures, college degrees, tribal beliefs, business titles, and family roles.

A common misconception is to tie your identity to something external or outside of yourself. Most often it is to your current role or title at work. If you are working long hours as the owner of your company, you identify as a business owner. If you've been climbing the corporate ladder for years, then the title of vice president, creative director, or CEO may be the identity you claim most often. If you are neck-high in diapers and playdates, you may say your calling is to be a stay-at-home mom. If you are standing in front of a classroom every day, you identify as a teacher.

But these are roles or jobs. They do not define us or fully represent who we are; they only represent things we do, even if those things are of great importance. The danger lies in putting our identity in a designation with a shelf life. When the role or title no longer fits, we can be left feeling adrift. We sell our company, we get laid off, choose to retire, the children leave home, and all of a sudden, we become rudderless because we've defined ourselves with a temporary title.

When I made the bold move to resign from my job at HGTV, it was met with much disbelief and disappointment. There were not many in my life who thought the choice was a wise one. The most repeated comment made to me was, "But this is who you are." I was, in the eyes of so many, a television executive or more broadly, I was HGTV.

Admittedly, this was the scariest part of leaving that world. The idea that I would wake up empty, with no identity. How much of my self-worth was in my job title or name of my company? In my head, I knew I was more than those words on a paper, but in my heart I wasn't so certain. I was also walking away from a huge salary and some pretty grand perks.

I began to wonder how much of my identity was wrapped up in my financial freedom. I began to wonder—was the foundation of my identity built on quicksand? If I wasn't those things, then who was I?

After much soul searching and reflection, I found that my truest identity was rooted in a purpose found in the internal, not the external. Something unshakeable, undeniable, and solely me. Ultimately, I discovered my job was what I did, not who I was.

You Are Unique

Fingerprints are set in stone by the time an unborn baby reaches seventeen weeks. The ridge pattern development on your fingertips depends not only on genetic factors but also on unique physical conditions. Fingerprints are so unique in their development that even identical twins who are genetically similar do not have the same prints!

> *"What lies behind us and what lies before us are tiny matters compared to what lies within us."*
>
> **—RALPH WALDO EMERSON**

Fingerprints are just one indicator that we all are uniquely created. It is one of the most fascinating characteristics of the human race. But it seems to be harder for us to believe that we are uniquely created internally as well. Many people I coach acknowledge they are successful but have trouble believing they are much different than the next successful person.

Articulating our identity through our own eyes is a stabling exercise. It starts within and is an expedition of self-exploration. The goal of the expedition is to define our uniqueness and sketch out our internal fingerprint. It will ensure that we create a Life Compass that is distinct to us, allowing our identity to remain consistent throughout the remainder of our life.

Quitting my job stripped away my titles and forced me to dream and explore the possibilities my unique self could offer the world. It took me off the stage, relieving me of my duties as the overachiever, the successful one, the restorer of peace and happiness, and one of my biggest roles at the time, HGTV executive.

Could I have gotten through my whole life without this discovery? Yes, many people do. Would I have continued to be successful and somewhat impactful? Probably. But I would have still been missing the full map that reveals a much more expansive existence.

Understanding and believing I was uniquely created for a purpose that could be manifested in different ways, through diverse careers, and at varying impacts gave me hope for an exciting future beyond any one role. Understanding and embracing more fully who I am has enabled me to create a Life Compass that belongs to me, giving me confidence to make bold choices I never imagined I would.

Just like a typical compass works by detecting the earth's magnetic field, our Life Compass works by detecting what each of us is naturally pulled toward. If you're ready to stop feeling lost in your story and start moving in the direction of the life you want, let's explore the four core questions that will unlock and activate the most valuable tool for your journey: your Life Compass.

UNIQUE TALENTS: WHAT ARE YOU BEST AT?

Analytics and advisory company Gallup International has created one of the most popular employee engagement surveys in the business. A key question in the survey is "At work, I have the opportunity to do what I do best every day." According to Gallup's research, "one of the most powerful strategies for managers and organizations is giving their employees opportunities to apply the best of their natural selves (their talents) as well as their skills and knowledge. As the leading attribute employees look for in a new job—and its absence is one of the main reasons employees leave a job—when people get to do what they do best every day at work, the organizations they work for get a boost in employee attraction, engagement and retention." [27]

When coaching employees and managers, I have found that this question stops many in their tracks, as they haven't fully considered what their best talents are, never mind if they are using them daily. Discovering and articulating these talents can be a key to raising your productivity and engagement at work and in your life.

We are each born with a few unique talents. When you exercise those talents during your life, they become strengths and allow you to shine. Unique talents are not just what you are good at but what seemingly comes naturally to you and you've become *best* at. You can see that they clearly exist in you, while they may not exist in others. You might not even be certain how you perform the talent; you were just born with that ability.

These talents are your best skills in relation to all the other abilities you have. There are many overachievers who can name several things they are *good* at, but I am looking for what you are *best* at. This is what Gay Hendricks calls our Genius Zone, or Tom Roth, author of *StrengthsFinder 2.0*, calls *dominant talents* or *strengths*. These talents are life-giving, filling you with energy when you are in the zone of using them. They are skills you love honing and improving upon. These talents tap directly into your inner motivations and tend to show up everywhere in your life.

Everyone around you would agree you excel at these skills. They are recognizable to many, especially those who work or live with you. Therefore, it is most helpful to reflect on the abilities and characteristics that your colleagues, family, and friends say you possess. We must humbly consider the compliments or positive feedback that we receive most often. We must not define our talents in a vacuum but seek honest consultation. Taking time out to discuss with those closest to you will help you create a list of talents that truly define how you best contribute to your world.

I worked in television and advertising for over twenty years, yet if you asked me what I was undoubtedly good at, I don't think the first thing out of my mouth would have had anything to do with the television or advertising industry. It was only when I looked more deeply at what I found the most pleasure in at work and in my personal life, rather than merely the daily tasks of my role, that

I could clearly articulate my innate gifts. I also pulled out past performance reviews, asked my friends and family, and reflected on any compliment I had received over the years. I also completed several helpful and statistically valid assessments, including StrengthsFinder 2.0[28] and The Motivation Code Assessment (MCODE).[29] While StrengthsFinder was helpful in understanding what I am good at doing, MCODE helped me articulate what drives me. It explained the why behind what I love to do. Todd Henry, author of *The Accidental Creative* and Chief Creative Officer at Pruvio, owner of the MCODE, told me, "We like to think of Motivation Code as the 'base layer' of self-knowledge. Understanding what truly drives your decisions, your instinctual behaviors, and your moments of deep gratification illuminates patterns in your life and work that can then be leveraged for personal growth and effectiveness." Utilizing such powerful assessments like these was beneficial in helping me land on key words to describe my talents.

Looking at repeated adjectives and nouns, I was able to piece together talents that I felt rang true to me. I believe these talents reflect my best contribution. I defined for myself my unique talents:

- **Influential Communicator:** I find the stage a natural fit for me and where I can project influential ideas.
- **Entrepreneurial Visionary:** I envision new, dynamic enterprises daily that will make a positive impact.
- **Strategic Advisor:** I am a trusted and wise counselor to individuals and groups.

It took a great deal of curious soul searching and honest evaluation to get to these three key talents and their definitions. There are no job titles in my unique talents. No awards. No roles. None of them say mom or wife. They are solely crafted around my unique internal fingerprint. They point expressly to how I was designed and what has bubbled to the surface over these last fifty years. They highlight the real me—the most useful me.

Watching someone do something that doesn't fit their gifting is like watching someone try on an ill-fitting coat. We can all fall prey to too many opportunities and too many options. Knowing what I am best at has given me the freedom to let go of trying to do the things that don't suit me or bring me satisfaction. When we define our unique talents, we suddenly have a filter. This filter can help us adequately decide what we should and shouldn't do. It is one more coordinate for the GPS of our life—keeping us on the right path, happy, and fulfilled.

You should be able to see hints of your talents woven throughout the entire story of your life. They are part of the fabric of your life and have made work seem more like play. You may have always been good with numbers or able to write. You may have an eye for color or design. You may be a gifted artist or musically talented. You might like the stage or crafting a speech. You may be good with animals or know how to negotiate an argument to peaceful resolution.

When doing the exercise of naming and articulating your talents, you must also push beyond the skill of the task and ask questions around *why* you are best at doing them, along with what aspect of the talent brings you joy. What is it that you really like about design? What type of art are you gifted at creating and why? What do you enjoy about selling or marketing a product or service?

Push to the feeling or emotion behind the talent. What brings you fulfillment when you are leading people? What type of creative are you? Why are you drawn to a particular project again and again? Why do you need to be the leader? What about it brings you joy? What turns it from work to play? These questions start to form the uniqueness to your talents.

Uncovering your unique talents teaches you to not just see the potential and power in yourself but to also see it in others. I can't help but look for clues in the people who work with me and for me. Understanding that each person is unique helps me see that this world is not a competition. I can admire and celebrate others' successes. When I identify and name the innate gifts in others, it becomes an energy source for them. It is an excellent tool for motivation. I can see how an entire team can fit together to create something more powerful and beautiful. Helping a team of people recognize this creates a new level of freedom in the workplace.

Crafting your unique talents gives you ownership. It brings it into your consciousness. It fuels confidence because you can easily communicate to others what you are best at, what makes you different, and what makes you most useful. It helps you contribute in the right way but also helps you know when you *can't* help, or might not be the best fit for the task at hand.

Embracing unique talents is freeing because it allows me to be me and you to be you. It makes me more curious about other people and helps me see the world in a more positive light. Our unique talents are a gift. They are a gift to be discovered and shared. Treasure these gifts. Use them and invest in them, and you will get closer to a life of significance.

PASSIONS: WHAT DO YOU CARE ABOUT?

While our unique talents make it clear *what* we are best at, our passions, or what we care about, point toward *where* and *how* we might live those talents out. Our passions are how we dream of using our talents to impact the world around us. Those ways should give us energy, hence the word passion. Much like we feel passion in a romantic relationship, we should feel an energetic connection to how we are living out our talents and giftings.

The Latin meaning of passion is a willingness to suffer for what you love. It is from this original meaning that Christians famously refer to the Passion of Christ. His love for the human race led to His willingness to suffer for their salvation.

Over time this meaning has changed. Today it has morphed into the feeling of intense love for someone or something. It is the insatiable drive toward where we find the most satisfaction and enjoyment.

Understanding the original meaning of passion can be reorienting. Looking at what we do through the lens of both love and suffering points us in a clearer direction. What or who are you drawn to?

What would you love to do even if it was really difficult? What would you do if time and money were not an issue? There you will find an ignited passion that will make a difference in the lives of those around you.

Often, in our drive to success, we can bury passions. They were more clear to us as young adults, but we set them aside. It can seem a bit risky to follow something we love in exchange for something that can bring us money, recognition, power, or comfort.

Finding our passions in life involves connecting to our heart. We must dissect our heart, uncovering its desires, drives, and longings. This is easier said than done. There is plenty in the world around us to mask our true heart's desire. Therefore we must peel back the layers and dig deep.

Asking questions around what you would do if you had unlimited money or unlimited time helps illuminate your inner passions. Identifying the groups or causes we are drawn to or have the greatest affinity for can also help point us in the right direction.

While our unique talents are typically permanent, our passions can change over time. This is because what is most important to us can alter depending on stages in life, making defining our passion feel elusive and confusing. We feel like it should be obvious, and we become discouraged if it isn't. This is why decoupling the idea of talents from passions is such a helpful task. Embrace the idea that you may have a range of burning interests. Be curious and explore the corners of your heart to uncover what you honestly long for and love.

CORE VALUES: HOW DO YOU WANT TO BEHAVE?

You are hard-pressed to walk into any company and not come across their core values. I remember in 1995 when HGTV created its core values. They gave us a framework in which to work, live, and relate to each other and to our clients.

Our core values were inclusion, compassion, clarity, openness, humor, shared responsibility, work-life balance, and integrity. They were helpful in hiring and useful in firing. It gave us confidence in shaping the environment we wanted off-air in our offices and on-air to our viewers.

What Did You Do to My House?

Trading Spaces was a popular television show that burst onto the scene in 2000. Many people often tell me it was one of their favorite HGTV shows, not realizing it was never on HGTV. HGTV was initially offered the American format rights to the UK show *Changing Rooms* but passed on the licensing deal. The rights went to TLC, and *Trading Spaces* was eventually born. The producers created a provocative show with sometimes controversial designs, which often led to tears and tantrums. Homeowners didn't always like how their neighbors had chosen to transform their house. The epitome of this was illustrated during one of its most well-known episodes, where grass was glued to the walls of one of the renovated rooms. Predictably, the homeowners hated it.

While many television producers make intentional choices to create drama in their programs, HGTV chose a different route—one that aligned with our mission.

I'll never forget sitting in a meeting where the head of programming clearly stated, "The show may be a hit, but it isn't us. On HGTV every show has a happy ending." We were very certain about what we were creating. We knew what we valued and what our viewers valued. That clarity made programming decisions for the top programming executives easier.

HGTV took a lot of flak for not taking the rights to that show. Many critics say that HGTV passed on a fantastic ratings opportunity. In hindsight, I see the brilliance of restraint in HGTV's decision not to create the program that *Changing Rooms* and eventually *Trading Spaces* became. Even though it was a ratings juggernaut for TLC, we can say we stuck true to the integrity of who we were and what we valued most.

When people look back on their lives, regrets typically come from decisions they fell into, didn't take the time to process, or had no filter for knowing whether it was a good or bad choice. These decisions ultimately violated who they were at their core. Just as in business, there is power knowing your own core values. They provide boundaries, giving confidence and clarity to the right and wrong endeavors in your life.

The Truth Behind You

Our core values give structure to our lives. They give us order and help us navigate what comes our way, be it situations or people.

Our core values frame how we think and interact with the world around us.

Your core values are shaped by your character. Your character is the foundation of how you show up and lead your life. Core values are essential to our being; they are not aspirational or imagined. They should be our non-negotiables.

We have all been to a party and have met someone for the first time. Sometimes those new acquaintances rub us the wrong way. They leave us unnerved, but we can't quite say why. Most often it is because they have violated our core values.

Popular author and professor Adam Grant writes, "the events that make your blood boil reveal what matters most to you. Anger rises when your core values are in jeopardy. With reflection, it becomes a mirror for seeing your principles more clearly. With action, it becomes a map for making change to protect what you hold dear."

Naming and claiming your personal core values are powerful tools for finding and shaping your village of people, those who you want and need to invest in. They can be a filter for keeping toxic people at bay. Core values will help you decide what companies or organizations you want to work with or for.

One thing that has become clear to many people after the COVID-19 pandemic and tumultuous year of crazed politics and social unrest is where their values lie. The veil was lifted on how people truly feel and what they cherish most. For some, it was the first time they had the space to think through what they truly valued. For my husband and me, it opened the door to discuss with our children the important values of our family. We spoke about the definition of truth and how we see the world separately and collectively. We talked about our non-negotiables. We talked about the families we related to easily, those who might be harder to joyfully break bread with, and how to find compassion to bridge the differences. It was a fruitful exercise to name our values and commit as a family to our boundaries.

Writer and philosopher Ayn Rand said, "Happiness is that state of consciousness which proceeds from the achievement of one's values." When we aren't living our core values, we feel off-kilter, dishonest, and unhappy. When we are living up to the values we have defined for ourselves, we are more at peace and therefore happier.

As you consider your personal core values, here are some common examples.

CORE VALUES

☐ Creativity	☐ Empathy	☐ Growth
☐ Community	☐ Humor	☐ Loyalty
☐ Work Ethic	☐ Contribution	☐ Optimism
☐ Determination	☐ Authenticity	☐ Trust
☐ Equity	☐ Connection	☐ Integrity

CORE PURPOSE: WHY DO YOU EXIST?

Doing the hard work of defining your unique talents, current passions, and personal core values allows you to properly articulate your core purpose. Another way of putting it: Your unique talents are your *what.* Your passions are your *where.* Your core values are your *how.* Your core purpose is your *why.* It ultimately answers the key question to a significant life—why do I exist?

Answering this question with a single, well-crafted sentence is a powerful tool to give your personal and professional life meaning and joy. Articulating a single purpose statement is an effective way to solidify your "why" in your mind and give you a compass for the future.

A defined mission can also fill people with drive and ambition for something greater than themselves. It pulls us out of an individualistic, success-only mentality and pushes us toward a more collective view of the world. A lack of mission leads people to despair, dysfunction, and alienation. It is a personal purpose that gives us more solid footing and a clear avenue to connect to others. It also helps us find the wonderful satisfaction in being useful to all those around us. People tend to feel the very best about themselves when they give the very best of themselves to others.

Creating a Purpose Statement

Creating a purpose statement for yourself is an exercise that takes thought and patience in which you craft a sentence that is influenced by your story, talents, passions, and values. When drafting your statement, starting the sentence with the words "My purpose is to" or "I exist to" is an excellent starting point. Most people feel comfortable with a statement that is not more than twelve to fifteen words. Some people like it even shorter so they can easily remember it.

Much like a business strategic plan, your purpose statement is your mission and will serve as your North Star for the remainder of your journey. Therefore, it must feel personal, unique, and, most of all, like you. You must be excited and energized by the sentence. You must *love* your purpose statement. It needs to be a statement that withstands time and pressure.

A purpose statement combines the key verbs, adjectives, and nouns that make up who you are, what you are passionate about, and the way you hope to impact the world, and most specifically the people around you.

My personal purpose statement is "I exist to envision and communicate ideas that help people live to their fullest potential." This statement gets me out of bed every morning. It includes the words I love and that inspire me most.

It is my purpose statement that propelled me and gave me the determination to write this book. Referring to it and reading it often helped me follow through even on the most challenging days. My purpose also pops into my head when I'm struggling to connect or find direction on certain days.

> ***I know I will easily find joy if I seek opportunities that connect to my purpose.***

It makes sense that my most fulfilling moments are when I'm helping a friend figure out their next career move, or when I'm talking to one of my teenagers about what job she might find enjoyable.

Crafting a lasting and impactful purpose statement can feel arduous, but after all the reflection and work you have done to this point in the book, you have all the material you need to ensure a well-crafted statement. No matter your stage of life or current employment status, you should have a purpose statement. The only thing creating a purpose statement will cost you is time, but the payoff is immense.

People tend to fail because they lose their way. Put your statement above your desk, on the bathroom mirror, and in your daily journal to ensure you stay on track. Meditate on it or say it out loud each day. Speak it into fruition. Live it out and see your life change—significantly.

EMBRACING YOUR LIFE COMPASS

Something special happens when you discover more of who you are. You transform psychologically when you truly believe that you were uniquely designed and that design has a purpose. When you become deeply connected to that uniqueness, you can harness a power that can impact the world around you.

Here is where the secret to changed lives resides. It is a bit of a paradox. You would think that all this time and energy focusing on yourself would make you more narcissistic. But that is not the case. When you know yourself on a deeper level, you stop trying to fill the void and stop trying to prove yourself. You are known and become secure in that knowledge. You begin to crave using your newly harnessed purpose for others.

Loving yourself can be a tricky concept to navigate, especially if you've spent years seeing self-care as selfish, indulgent, or even just optional. We must all find that healthy balance of believing in who we are without feeding into an ego-driven, self-conceit or falling into an unhealthy pursuit of perfection.

This is always more complicated than it sounds because we humans tend to wrestle internally with a divided self. We exude confidence while harboring insecurities. Those insecurities create an insatiable hunger for external validation. And because we are social creatures, we can't deny how good compliments from others feel.

While crafting your Life Compass, you spent a great deal of time answering important questions about who you are. Now that you are more self-informed, consider this your invitation to a healthy self-love.

Self-validation is critical for maximizing our impact through our purpose. It's a tool to better honor, grow, and care for ourselves with kindness and generosity, which has tangible benefits to all areas of our lives. Once we weave together the divided parts of our inner selves, we can commit to exploring our full potential with active participation rather than passive acceptance.

However, if we want to thrive throughout life, we cannot survive on the collective agreement of others. We must train ourselves to develop, nurture, and even protect our ability to self-validate.

We strike internal gold when we make a commitment to loving who we are while having the humility to know that we are still a work in progress. Think of it like finally making friends with yourself.

It's important to note that not every day of our life needs to or will be filled with important, impactful events. It sounds exhausting just typing it. But pausing to craft a Life Compass can actually open up tremendous amounts of time, energy, and freedom. We wander less, waste less energy, and are able to find the space in our lives for impact. Purpose is an excellent filter to keep us from doing the things we don't care about or aren't good at doing. We understand where we are truly needed and show up well.

The one thing you have in your life for certain is you. You can only affect change in yourself and in the lives of others when you accept you. Know you. Love you. Own you. Be you.

So these big, scary questions aren't so scary after all. They just take time and effort to wrestle through. Once you articulate the answers you will be ready to embrace and incorporate them into your mind and heart.

As you get closer to imagining the future you want, it's helpful to take stock of your life from a 360-degree angle.

In the following chapters we will examine how we can live one full and balanced life by exploring our Life Zones, or areas of life that when prioritized allow us to flourish. They include our health, family, friends, community, and work. We will dive deep into each zone to discover what good health, strong relationships, connected communities, and meaningful work looks like and how they each feed into a significant life.

Reflections

- Take time to sketch out your Unique Talents, Current Passions, Core Values, and Purpose Statement.
- Are you committed to each part of your Life Compass and using it in all your Life Zones? If not, what are some changes you need to make to be in alignment with your Life Compass?

CHAPTER SEVEN

YOUR HEALTH

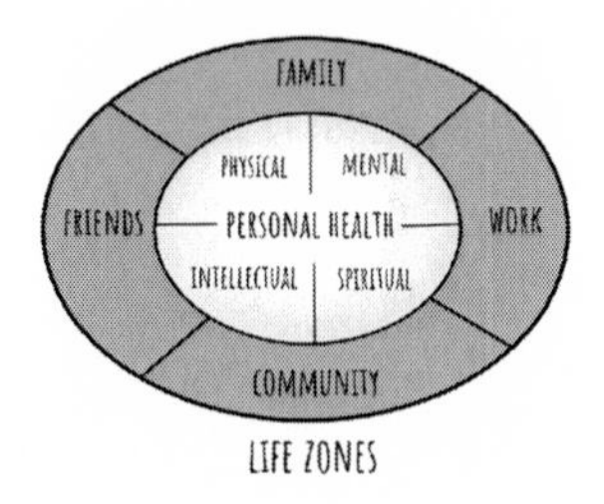

LIFE ZONES

"Accept responsibility for your life.
Know that it is you who will get you where
you want to go—no one else."

—LES BROWN

I'm standing in an airport desperately looking up at the departure monitor. After staring for a few minutes, it dawns on me. I'm not sure where I am or where I am going. It's television upfronts season, and I'm lost.

In the television industry, upfronts are when advertisers have a chance to buy large quantities of discounted advertising time on various networks up front, before the traditional fall season begins. Prior to negotiations, media companies make presentations, throw elaborate parties, and host events where they showcase their upcoming slate of fall programs and parade around top talent. From February to May, network executives meet internally to set strategy, decide how much inventory they hope to sell, and develop pricing models. Externally, they are traveling the United States to meet with key advertisers and host events in major cities.

It is May, and I've been on the road almost constantly for three months. I am participating in management strategy meetings in New York City, attending a nonstop slate of meetings with key advertisers, and leading upfront presentations across the country.

At the finish line of my meeting marathon was our premier event, the HGTV Dream Home Giveaway. Every year, HGTV gives away a fabulous home in some amazing location to one lucky winner. Once the winner is selected, we host an over-the-top event to present the beautiful home to the winner and thank the many wonderful advertising sponsors.

Exhausted and confused, I embarrassingly turned to a fellow traveler looking up at the board and asked, "I'm sorry, but what city are we in?"

I failed to remember that I was off to beautiful Maine to help give the HGTV Dream Home away. This was hands-down my favorite trip of the year, but this time, I did not want to go. Millions of people had entered this sweepstakes. Who wouldn't want to walk aimlessly through this beautiful house while sipping wine and talking to HGTV talent? Me, that's who. I was officially exhausted.

I longed for a quiet moment to get my head straight. I longed for my own bed. I longed for my family. I had not eaten well, slept well, or, evidently, managed my location well since February. My tank was empty.

YOUR OXYGEN MASK

Every time we board a flight, we listen to flight attendants share some variation of the Oxygen Mask Rule: "Should the cabin lose pressure, oxygen masks will drop from the overhead area. Please place the mask over your own mouth and nose before assisting others."

If the plane's oxygen level drops dangerously low and we mix up the order and help others with their mask first, we're likely to lose consciousness quickly. In other words, if we don't make putting on our mask our first priority, we won't be able to help anyone at all.

Recently, I pulled out an old journal to take myself back to this time in my life. In it I wrote,

> On the way home from the Dream Home in Maine we had a layover in New Hampshire. It was a windy day and the turbulence was awful. As we descended to land, our back tires hit the runway hard. Audible gasps from many passengers. We are going fast down the runway. Why isn't the nose of the plane going down? Why aren't we slowing down? We race down the runway, nose up, until... we take back off again. Back into the sky and the turbulence. The pilot comes on. "Sorry, folks, aborted landing. Too windy. We'll circle around and try again." I don't think there is enough money in the world to keep living like this.

While we didn't lose cabin pressure that day, I couldn't help but reflect on the idea of the oxygen mask. Had I lost my ability to care for myself properly? Was I putting the oxygen mask on all the other passengers in my life before putting it on myself?

In that turbulent moment, my body, mind, and spirit sure did feel like they were running out of oxygen.

Putting on your oxygen mask first can feel like a sharp left turn from how we are conditioned to show up in our circles. But most of us are living in bodies that are broken in some way. We are worn down physically due to a lack of care or depleted energy. We are living in high pressure worlds, with our mental and intellectual states constantly inundated with communications and messages due to technology. We are often stagnant, weak, sore, overpolluted, emotionally fractured, and spiritually empty. We aren't just in need of maintaining health; we are in need of healing our bodies.

The majority of Americans have type 2 diabetes or are prediabetic.[30] The majority! America is also the most medicated country in the world. One in two Americans takes prescription medication. Our healthcare system has become a sick-care system. While we are home to some of the best doctors and nurses, they are forced to do triage rather than spend their time optimizing people's health. Therefore, that job lies with us.

Henry Ford once said, "If you always do what you've always done, you'll always get what you've always gotten." If you want to finally get better, it's time to stop ignoring your health and put on your oxygen mask first.

The Work-Life Emergency

We've been told the best oxygen mask solution is to have work-life balance. The term *work-life balance* made its first appearance in the United States in 1986. Prior to that, the most used term was work-leisure time. There was a clear distinction between when you worked and when you did not. We had a clear time to punch into our jobs and a clear time to punch out. Everything outside our work time was deemed leisure time.

But times changed, with the 1980s epitomizing the "become all you can be" and "make as much as you can" philosophies. The climb to the top became the ideal journey—cue Michael Douglas in the 1987 movie *Wall Street* delivering the now famous line, "Greed is good." Work shifted from a means of production to a means to identity. This shift equated to Americans chipping their free time down by more than a third to just 16.6 hours a week.[31] The rise of digital technology in the 1990s and 2000s meant work was more accessible and became woven throughout every aspect of a worker's personal life as well. Using the term *work-life balance* was now a way to recognize the unweaving of the two. Can we have a life that isn't consumed by our work?

As I write this book, the idea of work-life balance seems like a complete myth. The COVID-19 pandemic and forced work-from-home requirements brought people face-to-face with their lives in a new way. We went from finding balance once we left our offices for home to never leaving home for the office. Now we are faced with the question of where work ends and life begins.

Pitting work against all other areas of life is a lose-lose situation. Instead of striving for the key to work-life balance, let's go all in on one, fulfilling, integrated life that maximizes our impact and our years.

> *"The first wealth is health."*
>
> —RALPH WALDO EMERSON

Fueling Our Health

Now that we have our Life Compass, we are able to find a new love and appreciation of our true selves. With that free mind and new appreciation, we can examine and address our personal health.

Understand that our capacity to live our best life correlates with what fuels our personal health—our energy. Discussions around balance tend to highlight the pressures on our time, but time-blocking your Google calendar isn't going to solve all your problems. If you are running on empty, an organized calendar isn't going to get you very far.

What we really need to focus on is where we receive our energy and how we are managing those sources. Our energy is fueled by our physical, mental, intellectual, and spiritual health. These natural energy tanks are the main sources of our life-giving oxygen. We all know that time is finite and fleeting. Finding more of it is a challenge for everyone. But managing our energy is a much more achievable goal.

I spend a significant amount of my coaching work helping people to slow down and take an inventory of their health. Many of my clients have not mastered the art of keeping their energy tanks full. Instead, they have become accustomed to spending much of their lives running on fumes. But doing this causes our physical body, mind, and spirit to suffer. We become tired, develop aches and pains, get sick with colds and migraines, or worse. We can fall into depression, develop autoimmune disorders, have heart attacks, or develop cancer. We drift and begin to feel disconnected from ourselves and those around us.

In other words, if our energy reserves are empty, not only will we be unable to live out our purpose and positively impact those around us, we may end up limiting our longevity. Once we create a lifestyle that is a constant renewable energy source, we become protective over our health, knowing that maintaining it is like oxygen to the body. Without it, we die.

A commitment to managing our physical, mental, intellectual, and spiritual health is the secret to maximizing our energy and in turn our personal well-being.

YOUR PHYSICAL HEALTH

Physical health is the first essential ingredient to unlocking optimal energy. It is the foundation to everything else we hope to accomplish or experience in life. Good physical health is obtained when your body is free from illness or injury. It includes having healthy organs, skin, dental health, weight, hygiene, and sleep. If you optimize your physical health, you can maximize your overall well-being.

Optimized physical health means an energetic and vibrant body. You feel like you have all the energy you need to fully engage with the day ahead of you. You feel a sense of strength and vitality.

We have already discussed how we have the *ability* to live longer than the generations before us but that is not a given. Longevity takes intentionality. Furthermore, living longer only becomes an attractive prospect when it means also being healthy.

But a twenty-first century life is riddled with unhealthy dietary options, sedentary lifestyles fed by on-demand streaming services, and a lack of sleep due to our hectic, success-driven schedules. Overwhelmed by so many options served up to us on how to approach diet and exercise, we abandon the menu altogether.

You do not fully understand why your grandparents kept saying, "At least you have your health," until you lose it. As we get older, a terrifying thing starts to happen. You hear news of friends, relatives, and famous people your age getting ominous diagnoses. This can cause an awakening to the truth that we have been given only one body. In large part, depending on how we treat it, that one body can either serve us or fail us.

Like our cars and homes, our bodies need upkeep and attention or they will age quickly and become unusable. Can you imagine how well you would care for your car if you were told it was the only one you would ever own? We would protect it from the elements, be certain it had the best fuel, and be sure it was receiving constant and consistent tune-ups. Are we giving that same thought and attention to the one and only body we will ever have?

The better way to manage your physical health is not to wait until you hear someone else's bad news or receive bad news yourself, but to care for your body now. We must break the patterns of yesterday that have crept into today and focus on a healthier tomorrow. The good news? The best and most repeated advice is to keep it simple.

The Physical Health Commitment

Human genetics haven't changed in thousands of years, but our lifestyles have, affecting our overall physical health in some dramatic ways. Our ancestors worked outdoors in the sun, hit the hay hard, slept deeply, and ate the fresh bounty from their harvests. Today, we work mostly indoors, sleep lightly, and eat processed and packaged food. We must commit to an overall shift. A proactive and intentional focus on our physical health can be achieved with three simple lifestyle habits; move more, eat well, and sleep better.

We are looking to first heal our bodies and then to continually optimize. We are not looking to train for the Olympics. If you ever overpromise yourself (hello, New Year's resolutions), you will always underdeliver. While we all know that physical health is essential, many do not embrace the reality that their life span is dependent upon it. Furthermore, most people do not realize that small changes go a very long way.

Take moving your body, for instance. Harvard University researchers recently noted that as little as fifteen minutes of physical activity a day can boost your life span by three years.[32] Surely, we can all commit to fifteen minutes of exercise for an extra three years of a healthy life! And that exercise does not need to be intense. In their book *Undo It!* Anne and Dean Ornish highlight how basic activities like walking, stretching, and lifting weights not only will help you maintain your physical health but can reverse heart disease, lower blood pressure, and reduce weight. Just going from sedentary to walking thirty minutes a day can cut premature death rates by 20 to 30 percent![33]

But we should continue to build and increase our level of activity as we get better at incorporating movement into our everyday lives. Dr. Dean Ornish writes in his book *Undo It!*,

> Exercise also lengthens your telomeres . . . telomeres are the structures at the ends of your chromosomes that regulate cellular aging. As your telomeres get shorter, your life gets shorter and the risk of premature death from just about everything increases correspondingly. People who have consistently high levels of physical activity have significantly longer telomeres than those who have sedentary lifestyles, and even longer than those who are moderately active.

Additionally, exercise releases endorphins, and those endorphins are shown to elevate our mood. A longer life is made even more attractive when we know it will be a happy one as well. So get moving and watch that smile appear.

Making simple changes to our diet can also add years to our lives. Interestingly, the word diet comes from the Greek word *dìaita*, which means lifestyle. Most doctors and researchers agree that fad diets are not the answer. You should slowly make small changes over a course of time to create a new and improved dietary lifestyle.

Functional medicine expert and bestselling author Dr. Will Cole states, "Eating foods that repeatedly don't love you back is like staying in a toxic relationship and wondering why you are so miserable. Avoiding the foods that do not love you back is a form of self-respect." We must examine our relationship with food and decide if what we are putting into our body is helping or hurting us. Just like with any relationship in our life, we must create healthy boundaries and commit to what will not only make us feel good but enhance our life span.

Harvard biologist David Sinclair wrote in his book *Lifespan* that having a diet consisting of at least 50 percent vegetables, increasing fatty fish, and reducing unhealthy carbs is key in extending our health span. While making all these changes may be too big of a leap for some, committing to one or two diet changes can make a significant difference.

It can seem like an uphill battle with the availability of unhealthy packaged goods and the temptation to eat sugary foods. Our foods are laced with ingredients that are toxic to our bodies. It takes intentionality to eat well. Again, the best way to thwart the temptation of attractive, bad food choices is to adopt a new mindset around healthy eating. This lifestyle should not feel like a punishment but instead be solely based on the idea that you want to feel good and enjoy a long life.

The last physical commitment you need to make is to your sleep. Many of us don't think too much about our sleep routine or understand the right routine for increasing longevity. Sleep is the time when our bodies do the majority of healing. Not getting enough sleep can lead to impairing our immune, cardiovascular, and nervous systems. It can also lead to an increased risk of obesity, diabetes, anxiety, depression, stroke, and even cancer.[34] A lack of good sleep can harm all areas of our health and deplete our energy to a point where the very worst version of ourselves appears.

But we aren't looking for too much sleep. What we need, like everything in life, is balance. In one groundbreaking study on sleep and mortality, researchers followed over 21,000 twins for more than twenty-two years. They asked questions about the twins' sleep habits and looked at their longevity. Researchers found that if people slept less than seven hours a night or more than eight hours a night, they had an increased risk of death (24 percent and 17 percent, respectively).[35] It seems everyone will benefit from a solid eight hours of good sleep.

While grabbing eight hours of good sleep a night seems like a simple charge, it is harder to achieve in our blue-light-ridden, fast-paced, and noisy world. Sleep specialist Dr. Bijoy John of the Sleep Wellness Clinics of America states, "We spend a third of our life in bed and the impact it has on the human body is dynamic and affects various organ systems. Once you get a good night's rest, your whole day is better and you become happier and more productive." Dr. John believes that 20–25 percent of our total sleep needs to be in the deepest state. This can be hard to achieve without good health and a bedtime routine. Creating a sleep routine by disconnecting earlier and getting ready for bed can be key to an optimal sleep experience, giving your brain a chance to rest and heal. Shutting down our electronic devices, cutting out late night snacks, and quieting our surroundings are necessary signals our body needs to receive in order to begin to relax and ready our mind to shut off. We also need a cool, dark, and quiet environment to keep the body at rest throughout the night.

We don't want to become overwhelmed by all of these helpful health suggestions. Again, adding small, impactful commitments in your weekly routine will lead to lifelong healthy habits. Pick the process, the diet, or the exercise program that you are most drawn to and that you can realistically maintain. Commit to setting an alarm to alert you when it is time to wind down for bed and wake up.

If you have the financial flexibility, consider going deeper. Consider investing in your physical health routine by signing up with personal trainers and making appointments to see nutritionists or functional medicine doctors. Getting ahead of any health issues as we age is much easier than trying to undo the damage once we receive a "bad news" diagnosis.

What Physical Health Means to Me

My view on my physical health was dramatically altered after my rheumatoid arthritis diagnosis. I was one of those people who wasn't awakened to the precious fragility of the human body until mine was in real distress. When I experienced the power of a holistic approach to medicine and physical care, I became obsessed with learning more.

My wellness journey over the last twenty-five years has been transformative and, believe it or not, fun. I have found there is power in a blended approach of both Western and Eastern medicine. Talking to many experienced and trusted doctors, learning about the practices of functional medicine, exploring Ayurvedic treatments, researching herbs and supplements, and understanding the power of clean, natural food has shaped my health today.

The number one thing I have learned is that you can find so much healing in the natural world around you. I have embraced all that nature has to offer. My very favorite place to shop is my local farmer's market. I find wandering from booth to booth feels therapeutic. Every Saturday morning becomes a lesson in what our earth can produce as I talk to the different vendors about their products and processes. I leave with fresh, organic food that will feed my body with the clean nutrition it longs for.

Increasing vegetables and fruits in my diet has flooded my body with isoflavones, antioxidants, bioflavonoids, and phytochemicals. While all of these big words may not make sense to me, I can't deny that I feel entirely different when I am committed to a healthy diet than when I'm living off processed foods. I also keep a gluten-free diet and avoid as much processed food as possible.

This doesn't mean there aren't times when I indulge. I love food and I love wine. I live my life in what I call an 80/20 routine. Eighty percent of the time I am very strict. Twenty percent of the time, I indulge my cravings. I will say over the years I more easily stick with the more stringent diet options because I simply feel better and have more energy. But knowing I can indulge when I feel like it is good for my mental attitude toward my nutrition and has allowed my diet to morph into a lasting lifestyle.

I also get out into nature. Going for long walks or hikes near my house has not only strengthened my body but restored my soul. Research shows that twenty minutes of walking reduces markers of inflammation,[36] which is critical for someone like me with an inflammatory disease. I've also included practices such as Pilates and hot yoga into my weekly routine.

One area of struggle for me has been my sleep routine. Stress coupled with a poor sleeping environment disrupted my sleep. It wasn't until I created a sleep routine that I saw my energy renewed. Drinking a cup of herbal tea and taking a warm bath each evening slows my body and mind down. Blackout curtains, a sound machine in the form of an air purifier, and lowering the thermostat set the stage for a deep, uninterrupted sleep.

These small changes and wellness habits have made a big difference in the health of my body and have increased my energy levels. But I'm not done. I have set a goal to continually reverse my biological aging process and eventually reverse my RA. My longevity mindset has fueled the lifestyle changes I have adopted in order to reverse my disease. I know I have additional commitments to make to get there, but I am ready and moving in the right direction.

YOUR MENTAL HEALTH

While it is commonplace to talk about eating healthy and going to a gym, we have a harder time acknowledging the needs of our brain and mind. Our mental health is defined as our emotional, psychological, and social well-being. It affects how we think, feel, and act. It also helps determine how we handle stress, relate to others, and make choices.

Optimal mental health is when your mind feels relaxed and calm. You feel an emotional sense of peace and can manage all your emotions with a clear head. You are absent of an overwhelming sense of anxiety or debilitating stress. Your mind feels strong and capable.

The journey to success often includes an increased amount of responsibility, which can compound the mental and emotional pressure in our lives. In this pressure cooker, it's likely that unresolved trauma and conflict have often been pushed down due to lack of time, energy, and possibly awareness to address and resolve. On top of what we have walked through in the past, we are faced with the constant onset of everyday stress. It should be no surprise then that the number one mental disorder in America is anxiety.[37] It is everywhere and can take a serious toll on our emotional well-being.

Stress is the number one repeated issue I hear from my clients. More than half of us say we are stressed on a daily basis. A 2021 Gallup study reports that 62 percent of working women say they are stressed daily, while 52 percent of working men say the same.[38] The struggle is real, and until we know how to manage it, we will suffer with mental health issues.

Poor stress management and coping skills are negatively affecting our minds and even shortening our lives. Studies show that it isn't just the presence of stress that shortens our telomeres but our body's ability to handle stress.[39] Those who are not physically and mentally healthy tend to absorb stress more and lack the ability to manage it properly. The research highlighted that it is not the amount of stress in our lives but our ability to navigate it that determines our stress levels.

These heightened stress levels have depleted our energy banks. Many have reached a point of complete exhaustion and even depression. More often than not, we can't even tie it to anything specifically. We have lost the ability to unravel the tangled web of stress and overcommitment. We are on autopilot and running on fumes.

The Mental Health Commitment

Dealing with stress, anxiety, and depression is no trivial matter, but there is good news. The heightened awareness of stress and mental health issues means we have a deeper understanding of what we are dealing with and how to best address the crisis at hand.

First, we must understand the difference between stress and anxiety. Stress is the body's natural response to a threat. Human beings are hardwired to react when we see the lion running in our direction. We either stay and fight the lion or we turn and run for our lives. This is a human being's innate fight-or-flight response.

Anxiety is our body's response to stress. It is a persistent and excessive worry that will not go away even after the removal of the stressor. While stress is caused by external factors, anxiety is internal. Knowing this difference helps us understand how to best address each of them in our lives.

While some stress in life is natural and even useful, a constant state of stress means we are experiencing external threats repeatedly and can be very unhealthy. We must change our situation or remedy the threat. This could mean exiting a toxic work environment, terminating a bad business partnership, or ending an abusive marriage. It could mean altering a relentless work schedule or ridding our calendar of unnecessary commitments. If we don't end the threat, the stress will remain, and eventually our body and mind will pay the consequences.

If our stressors are gone and the anxiety remains, then it is time to deal with the internal issues plaguing our mind. I call it minding the anxiety gap. This gap usually exists because we have fixated on some future escape or cannot let go of some past issue.

Spiritual teacher Eckhart Tolle discusses how this gap can best be managed by examining our thoughts and reorienting ourselves to live in the present.

> All negativity is caused by an accumulation of psychological time and denial of the present. Unease, anxiety, tension, stress, worry—all forms of fear—are caused by too much future, and not enough presence. Guilt, regret, resentment, grievances, sadness, bitterness, and all forms of nonforgiveness are caused by too much past, and not enough presence.[40]

We must manage the reflex to escape to a preferred, imagined future or remedy the negative fixation on an unfortunate past experience. When we learn to embrace a healthy present, we are then able to reduce the anxiety that plagues us.

This is easier said than done, at least if you try to go it alone. For those clients dealing with trauma or emotional issues, I always suggest seeing a professional, licensed counselor as part of their comprehensive mental health plan. Many of us need a personal trainer to effectively help us achieve our physical health goals. The same is true for our mental health. A therapist can help strengthen our minds by resolving past trauma and developing healthier habits for handling stress and anxiety in the future.

If you are wrestling with how to eradicate those threats or stressors, a qualified executive coach can help you best strategize your next move.

Living a significant life may include considering the greater good and connecting more fully to those around us, but it doesn't mean fulfilling everyone else's needs and dreams. People pleasers and over-givers can become overwhelmed by the idea of living out their purpose in a full and connected way. They may mistakenly believe that it means they must say yes to everything, or continually give.

Dr. Henry Cloud, author of the bestselling book *Boundaries*, states, "There is a direct correlation with people who are out of control in their lives and their hatred of the word 'no'." I encourage you to use your Life Compass as a permanent filter on what you are called and not called to do. Not only is saying no an acceptable response in most circumstances, it is a prerequisite for mental wellness, which is inseparable from living a life of significance.

Mental health can also be optimized through a number of different mindfulness practices. Mindfulness, translated from the Pali word *sati* (Sanskrit: *smrti*), literally means "to remember." Mindfulness pioneer Jon Kabat-Zinn defined it as "paying attention in a particular way: on purpose, in the present moment and non-judgmentally."

Meditation is a well-known and widely accepted practice of mindfulness. Alternative medicine specialist Deepak Chopra states, "Meditation is not a way of making your mind quiet. It is a way of entering into the quiet that is already there."

Creating space and time to enter that quiet and be still is a gentle way to calm and reset your brain, giving it the best chance to tackle stress. Quietly emptying your mind and then focusing on a life-affirming mantra is a prevalent form of meditation. Using apps to help guide you through a short time of meditation is another way to adopt the practice into your daily routine.

Dr. Daniel Amen, a brain specialist and board certified psychiatrist, suggests adding diaphragmatic breathing exercises in the morning and at night.[41] Take a deep breath from your diaphragm, hold it for four seconds and then release it for another six seconds. You can do it several times a day or anytime you need to reduce stress and reset the brain.

Millions of people are suffering from poor mental and emotional health. Millions more are drowning in a sea of daily stress and anxiety. We must commit to being in a healthy relationship with our brains and recognize our body's need to slow down. To maintain strong mental health, we must be able to access and reset our emotions.

We must allow ourselves time and space to be still, think, process, and dream.

What Mental Health Means to Me

For my parents' and grandparents' generation, the idea of mental health and the need for mental practitioners was a taboo subject. I was raised with a "pick yourself up by the bootstraps" mentality. While stigma around mental health remains today, the environment to discuss and explore mental health issues is much more open.

It wasn't until my twenties when I decided I might see a therapist for the first time. Life was going at lightning speed, work stress was increasing, and I was suffering regret from a recent breakup. I remember the relief I felt after my first therapy session. All I did was talk to a stranger about my life. Why did it feel so good?

Being alone in our thoughts can be a confusing and sometimes even scary place to reside. Our thoughts can often take on a life of their own, moving us in a more negative and destructive direction. Bringing those thoughts into the light, in the safe environment of a therapy room, is sometimes all that is needed to eliminate negativity and regain our footing.

I became so intrigued by human psychology and the power of the mind that I began to read a number of books on the subject. Around the height of my insatiable curiosity, I was promoted at HGTV to oversee my current division. With it came increased management responsibilities. While the network was growing at a rapid pace, we did not yet have a fully developed human resources department nor a ready management training program. The idea of an MBA wasn't attractive to me, but the thought of a master's of psychology seemed like it might remedy two needs: my appetite for learning about the human mind and my need to become a good manager of people.

On nights and weekends over the course of the next three years, I completed my master's of professional psychology. I learned the various theories around mental health and also the practical, clinical skills necessary to meet people where they are. I became better equipped to listen well and decipher the often unsaid needs of my employees. It was just the training I needed to become an effective and present manager.

Even with all my training, I didn't have what I would call a heart-and-head connection around mental health until after the birth of my second child. I was extremely excited to have another baby. I loved motherhood, and growing our family was a welcome blessing.

Shortly after giving birth to my daughter, I was plagued with an overwhelming sense of depression. I felt disconnected from her and the world around me. I vacillated between crying at the drop of a hat and feeling absolutely nothing at all. It was as if a dark cloud was hovering over my head with no clear escape. I was baffled. There was no reason to feel this way. My circumstances were not dictating my depression.

At a follow-up doctor's visit, I was told I was suffering postpartum depression. I had studied this in school, but to experience it was a whole other ball of wax. Understanding fully the lasting effects of an attachment disorder, I spent countless hours holding my baby on my bare chest and whispering how much I loved her despite the disconnect of those words from my mind. My doctor told me that it should lift during the traditional eight-week hormone shift, but he would start me on medication if it did not.

At eight weeks, as if on cue, I awoke one morning as if a veil had been lifted. I noticed the sun was shining and picked up my daughter with a full and happy heart. I was one of the lucky ones. I came through. I was also blessed with one of the most educational experiences of my life. No longer did I look at people with chronic depression and wonder why they couldn't just get it together. I understood what chemical imbalance really meant and felt like. I understood that sometimes, regardless of how perfect your surroundings may seem, life can feel unbearable.

For me as a manager and eventually a practitioner, it was a gift I will be forever grateful to have been given. A gift of empathy for those who truly suffer and see no way out.

> ***Empathy is the key to understanding mental health, in yourself and others.***

I didn't know that all of this would lead me to where I am today. A place where I combine my corporate business experience with my psychology training every day, walking alongside clients to help them better navigate their worlds. It is a rich working environment that I enjoy immensely, reminding me daily of the fragility of our mental health and the importance of committing to maintain its strength.

YOUR INTELLECTUAL HEALTH

For some, the idea of including intellectual health as part of your overall well-being is a bit foreign. But focused time on caring for our intellectual health is essential to creating, innovating, and thinking critically. In other words, it's a key part of a significant life.

Intellectual health is recognizing one's creative abilities and finding ways to expand your knowledge and skills.

Optimal intellectual health is a commitment to lifelong learning. It is an openness to new ideas and experiences in all areas of your life. You feel like your brain is continually expanding and being maximized.

Our brain is the most powerful yet underutilized organ in the human body.[42] Because we don't understand how to maximize the health of our brain, we are not benefiting from the power that lies within us.

For many of us approaching or enjoying our middle-age years, the conversation around intellectual health can be a scary one. Remembering where I put my keys or even what I wore yesterday seems to be a little harder than it used to be. Rather than buying into the idea that our brain cells are evaporating at a rapid rate and our sharp-as-a-tack days are behind us, we can increase our intellectual health by leaning into our brain ability and capacity.

The Intellectual Health Commitment

One of the most fascinating aspects of the brain is neuroplasticity—the brain's ability to change and adapt as a result of experience. The brain has the capacity to reorganize pathways, create new connections, and even produce new neurons. We must drive this neuroplasticity within ourselves and point it in a healthy direction.

According to cognitive neuroscientist Dr. Caroline Leaf, "The brain is the only organ in the body that gets better with age, but there is a caveat: It needs to be used properly."[43] There are several ways we can ensure that our brain gets better with age.

First, we must commit to learning something new. Margie E. Lachman, a psychologist at Brandeis University who specializes in aging, states, "Education seems to be an elixir that can bring us a healthy body and mind throughout adulthood and even a longer life."[44] Dr. Lachman also touts that continued education is associated with a decreased risk of dementia.

Thankfully, there are many ways we can support continued education through the second half of life. Expanding beyond education in our vocational craft is also essential to broaden our worldview. Creating a list of books to read, podcasts or seminars to listen to, or conferences or retreats to attend is a great way to commit to the learning journey. These activities, while great for expanding the brain, are also healthy ways to disconnect from mindless entertainment or stressful work.

Many of us are not losing our memory due to age but rather our inability to slow down and allow our brain to process. When we are stressed, we have a more difficult time creating short-term memories.[45] You may not be able to remember that dentist appointment because an overwhelmed workday has precluded you from logging it into your short-term memory bank.

Slowing down to simply daydream or journal your daily thoughts each and every day is a great way to protect and grow your brain. Dr. Leaf suggests you can engage the 200 different sections of the brain simply by allowing your mind to wander. "Walk and immerse yourself in a conversation with your own mind, noticing all the details of everything around you," she suggests. Resist pointing your mind in any specific direction. Let go and see where your mind takes you.

Research shows that none of us are fully left- or right-brained, which means we all have the ability to be creative. While only some people may be gifted in the arts, everyone can, at the very least, appreciate or learn about the creative aspects of our world. Listening to music, going to the theater, or visiting an art gallery are all ways to expand our knowledge and appreciation of the artistic world around us. If you've always wanted to learn an instrument or to sing, paint, draw, or do pottery, it is never too late. Our brain is ready to create new pathways and take in new information.

Another key to intellectual health is staying curious. Intellectual growth reminds us that we do not know all there is to know and most likely never will. This is one of the most exciting parts of human existence. The idea that there is no bottom. There is always another perspective to see, more history to learn, or another story to hear. Those new experiences will broaden our minds and deepen our empathy. Intellectual growth expands our vision—for ourselves, our families, our friends, and ultimately our society.

What Intellectual Health Means to Me

Music has always come naturally to me. Never shy on a stage, I have felt rather comfortable standing before a crowd singing into a microphone. I love the feeling I have when I sense the music flowing through me. I feel safe with music. It brings me comfort and peace.

When I was in my twenties, I learned to play the guitar—not very well, but well enough to accompany myself during a song or two. As I aged and eventually had children, the guitar gathered dust in the corner. It wasn't until my late thirties that I decided to pick it up again. Much to my dismay, my left hand could not form the necessary shapes to play guitar chords. The birth of my children had caused a resurgence in my rheumatoid arthritis, resulting in a slightly stiffened and reshaped hand. I felt heartbroken. Not only could I not do something I loved, but I was reminded once again of a dreaded limitation in my body.

Discussing this with a musician friend of mine, he simply looked at me and said, "You know there are several famous left-handed guitar players: Jimi Hendrix, Paul McCartney, Kurt Cobain. Why don't you learn to play the guitar with your good hand?" My first response was that I was too old. Why would a forty-year-old woman with a full-time job and small children decide to relearn to play the guitar?

After further encouragement, I decided to take a class at the famous Old Town School of Music in Chicago. At first it felt like my brain was cramping. The chords were all backward and upside down in my head. It was hard to strum with any natural rhythm with my left hand, but my teachers were supportive and excited to see me trying something so unusual. It wasn't every day they saw someone relearning guitar with their nondominant hand. But there was something else that was new to me: the school was filled with people my age, excited to learn instruments, sing, and dance. The lobby and sitting areas were littered with people practicing, chatting, and drinking coffee. People were writing songs and putting bands together.

I felt alive and young again. Learning something new, stretching my brain, and immersing myself in a creative environment was invigorating. Once again, my limitation had a silver lining. I chose to embrace that opportunity and create a new pathway in my brain. It was a launching pad for my intellectual growth throughout my forties and into my fifties. I find myself looking for new ways to stretch myself. I've recently decided to learn Spanish again. Growing up in South Florida meant an entire childhood learning the language. I let it slide but am now excited about diving in again. I subscribe to health and longevity podcasts and have shelves of books that keep my mind vibrant. Because I have decided to live into my hundreds, I know that I have a lot of time left to fill the neuropathways of my brain. I have embarked on a journey to grow my most powerful organ, keeping me sharp as a tack for the years to come.

YOUR SPIRITUAL HEALTH

While spirituality may mean many different things to many different people, in general, your spirit is the part of you that naturally journeys to connect to something bigger than yourself. To believe in your spirit is to believe there is something more to you than just a physical body. Often that recognition in your spirit or soul leads to a faith in a higher power or being. Many people ultimately make a very conscious decision to be tethered to something or someone greater than themselves. This is their spiritual life.

> *"The place God calls you to is the place where your deep gladness and the world's deep hunger meet."*
>
> **—FREDERICK BUECHNER**

Optimal spiritual health is a shift from a reliance on yourself to a reliance on something greater. It is a feeling of connection and groundedness. It is this vulnerable grounding that enables us to rest in our unique talents and purpose, using them to impact the world around us rather than using them in constant pursuit of comfort and indulgence. When we maximize our spiritual health, we feel lighter and more joyful.

Spirituality rings more true when it is not overly pious or legalistic in nature. It also appears to hold more validity when it is not completely vague or ambiguous. You can be very religious and not be living a life of faith, but one that is instead wholly connected to adhering to laws of doctrine, disconnected from your soul—doing good to look good or in order to earn something. This is a religion ultimately focused on yourself. Or you can call yourself spiritual and have no religion but seem to be floating, hoping to one day connect to something real. Neither journey seems to have reached its true destination.

Spirituality can be a difficult concept to grasp, especially for those who have achieved much through a reliance on self and the pursuit of success. For many of the highly successful people I coach, the idea of having faith or a faithful spiritual practice seems ambiguous at best and confining at worst.

Many successful people aren't sure they need belief in anything outside of themselves. They have done just fine without it. Some people have been burnt by religion or religious people. Some are wary that spirituality will cause them to lose themselves or sacrifice the comforts they've grown to love.

Spirituality or faith today can seem completely elusive to many because the human race became somewhat disconnected from religion in the twentieth and twenty-first centuries. Because of the enormous suffering through great wars and unforgettable financial depressions, many came to believe that God is absent or aloof. The traditional way of thinking "do good and you will have a good life" or "do bad and you will be punished" faded away. With the rise of evil people like Hitler, Stalin, and Mao, and the slaughter of 200 million people or more, the shift went from dependence on the spiritual to dependence on the self.

Over time, this has led to a very self-centered, individualistic society with a "what is best for me" mentality. We have lost sight of the benefit and ultimate fulfillment we can feel in a soul-filled and soulful spiritual health mindset.

Perhaps you embraced the "strive without ceasing" mentality and it served you well in your quest for success. You have worked diligently on your own to earn a place of worthiness. However, I have a feeling that worthiness has come at a cost, leaving you exhausted and unfulfilled. Maybe you like the idea of having spiritual health and just need some help on why and where to start.

The Spiritual Health Commitment

Clinical psychologist and researcher Dr. Lisa Miller examined the power of spirituality in her book *The Awakened Brain*. Her research team compared the brain structures of depressed and nondepressed people and cross-referenced them with those who described spirituality or religion as high importance or low importance. They wanted to see how spirituality was associated with brain structure and if there was any correlation with a risk for depression. She describes the exciting results of the study.

> The high-spiritual brain was healthier and more robust than the low-spiritual brain. And the high-spiritual brain was thicker and stronger in exactly the same regions that weaken and wither in depressed brains... Spirituality appeared to protect against mental suffering.

They say faith can move mountains. It appears that it is a major component to keeping our bodies and minds healthy as well. Science aside, those with strong spiritual health often testify it is this deep grounding that gets them through the hard times and provides essential strength to keep going. When we hold a strong belief that someone greater will guide us to something greater during our times of need, that belief becomes a light post illuminating the darkest parts of our journey.

Having optimal spiritual health can be a rudder in a chaotic world. It can help us make sense of it all. It gives us meaning, solidifies our purpose, and restabilizes us in times of stress and anxiety. Having a spiritual anchor allows us to let go of the reins a bit more and trust that there is meaning behind what is happening, even if it is not apparent to us. It doesn't just keep us on course but helps us survive the course.

Viktor Frankl survived a Nazi concentration camp and went on to write the seminal book *Man's Search for Meaning*. His survival, he came to find, was dependent on more than just his physical endurance. It was spiritual health that turned out to be the key to survival.

> In spite of all the enforced physical and mental primitiveness of the life in a concentration camp, it was possible for spiritual life to deepen. Sensitive people who were used to a rich intellectual life may have suffered much pain (they were often of a delicate constitution), but the damage to their inner selves was less. They were able to retreat from their terrible surroundings to a life of inner riches and spiritual freedom. Only in this way can one explain the apparent paradox that some prisoners of a less hardy makeup often seemed to survive camp life better than did those of a robust nature.

Frankl went on to write and speak about how spiritual beliefs make it easier for people to find true meaning. He believed that humans' ultimate goal in life should not be to pursue money or happiness but to pursue that meaning. "We should above all else understand the purpose of our lives."

Committing to optimal spiritual health is not about losing agency in your life. It's not all about self-sacrifice and weakness, nor is it about the confines of endless laws and judgment. Spirituality can be a transformation to a higher truth that empowers you to live a life free from the unhelpful and destructive ways of your old life and reliant on a love that transcends this natural world. Ultimately, it changes the way you look at yourself, others, and the world around you because it expands your view beyond this world and into the eternal. A healthy spiritual life helps us connect more fully to our purpose and belief in our unique design.

What Spirituality Means to Me

As a successful person, finding faith in God was the deepest and most lasting way to pull me out of a life in pursuit of my own glory and put me on a path to a life of deeper purpose in serving, connecting, and lifting up others. My spiritual life is grounded in Christian beliefs. After much soul searching, I've found Christianity both rationally and intellectually sound. It is emotionally satisfying to me, which creates a path for my heart, mind, and soul to be fully connected to God. I find that I am secure and at peace in my faith.

My spiritual life has found its grounding in a belief in one higher power. I believe in one God, who created the world and uniquely created me. It is Him I serve and the world around me that He created.

While that commitment may seem confining or narrow-minded to some, it turns me outward and opens up a vast world beyond the confines of myself. It frees me from the identity traps and the exhausting job of trying to prove myself to everyone.

> *"And now that you don't have to be perfect, you can be good."*
>
> **—JOHN STEINBECK**

My faith is best described by a quote from theologian and author Tim Keller: "We are more sinful and flawed in ourselves than we ever dared believe, yet at the very same time we are more loved and accepted in Jesus Christ than we ever dared hope." I find this to be one of the truest definitions of grace. Having a spirituality that is rooted in this kind of grace has given me a peace that passes all understanding. It humbles me in a way that allows me to be accepting of others, regardless of their background or status. It also opens me up to the idea of deeper community, and to loving myself and those around me with a strength beyond my own.

Ultimately, having a deep and connected spiritual life gave me the courage to leave my high-powered job for a new adventure. I rested in the knowledge that my identity was in something greater than my fancy work title. I also continue to find my faith brings me a contentment that money cannot buy. Resting in complete reliance on God, His love, and the belief that He created me with and for a purpose is the ultimate peace.

CREATING LASTING CHANGE

In the bestselling book *The Power of Habit*, author Charles Duhigg introduces the idea of Keystone Habits. These are habits that will disrupt and influence other habits. He writes, "Keystone habits say that success doesn't depend on getting every single thing right, but instead relies on identifying a few key priorities and fashioning them into powerful levers... The habits that matter most are the ones that, when they start to shift, dislodge and remake other patterns ... Small wins have enormous power, an influence disproportionate to the accomplishments of the victories themselves." It is time to take small, impactful steps to make long-lasting positive change in your life.

While I've made some helpful suggestions in this chapter on a few simple practices you can adopt, this is hardly an exhaustive list. I encourage you to do your own research and think carefully about your own body. Visit your doctor and discuss a plan that would work best for you. Carefully craft a list of the practices that will optimize all areas of your personal health and execute it daily.

Breathing in a life of significance in a world in constant chaos doesn't work without putting your oxygen mask on first. Prioritizing your personal wellness is a lifelong commitment that makes you more fit for your purpose. You wouldn't climb Mount Everest without preparing for the experience. Optimizing your personal health is essential for the journey toward achieving your vision. We must do this without apologizing or justifying to those around us. We must stop making excuses for our lack of commitment. We must stop neglecting what we know to be true. If we don't, we will only exist in some expired comfort zone that leaves us running on fumes.

Our relationship with ourselves is arguably the most important one we will ever have. If this relationship isn't healthy, then it is likely our other relationships will suffer as well. Do not take the health of your physical body, your mind, or your spirit for granted. As we age, we have less runway to heal and reverse the damage we've accumulated. The time to commit to your health is now. Push through the discomfort and take up the challenge of a healthier life. Put on your oxygen mask first. It's a matter of life and death!

Reflections

- Consider each area of your Personal Health: Physical, Mental, Intellectual, and Spiritual. Rate each area on a scale from 1-5 (5 being optimal).
- Make a list of the activities that could improve your score for each category. The list can include aspirational activities with the hope that you will commit to them in the future.

CHAPTER EIGHT

YOUR VILLAGE

"Let us be grateful to the people who make us happy; they are the charming gardeners who make our souls blossom."

—MARCEL PROUST

I remember when the movie *Cast Away* was released in 2000. Like most of my friends and colleagues, I went to see it during opening weekend, and we were all taken by the blockbuster's strong yet simple tale of survival.

As you may remember, Chuck Noland, played by Tom Hanks, is an obsessively punctual FedEx employee who finds himself stranded on an uninhabited island in the South Pacific where time stands still. When his efforts to set sail and search for help fail, Chuck attempts to orient himself by creating shelter and finding food. In the most memorable scenes, we also watch him feed his need for connection and belonging through conversations with his handmade volleyball friend, Wilson.

Initially, when Chuck began conversing with Wilson, you may have thought he just needed to get the thoughts in his head out into the open. But in one pivotal moment when Chuck wakes to discover Wilson had floated across the ocean and out of his reach forever, we grasp how essential human companionship is to Chuck's survival. The immense pain of losing what he came to see as a true friend was heart-wrenching for even the most cynical viewer. I've never been able to look at a volleyball the same again.

Chuck's desperate companionship with a personified volleyball reminds us that we were not designed to navigate this world alone. Just as we took the time to work on our relationship with ourselves, we must turn outward to look at the people around us. If we truly want to survive and thrive in our years to come, let's look at what it takes to intentionally grow and optimize the health of our relationships.

THE VITAL BENEFITS OF GOOD RELATIONSHIPS

There is such beauty in human relationships. It is where we can experience true authenticity, meaningful connection, and profound change and growth in ourselves and others. Healthy relationships help us realize the power of true service and investment in future generations. The survival of our human spirit depends on meeting our needs for connection and belonging.

But for many highly driven people, their quest for success can place a wedge between realizing a dream and having deeply connected relationships. Maintaining strong and healthy relationships takes consistent effort and work.

I'd like us to look at our relationships in two ways. First, that they are necessary for a long and healthy life. Second, relationships are essential for a significant life.

Human beings are social species, and it makes sense that having social relationships affects our overall health. Research shows that healthy relationships can add years to our lives by reducing stress levels, warding off depression and suicide, and lowering the risks of dementia, heart disease, and cancer, as well as boosting our immune system.

In fact, science journalist Marta Zaraska writes in her book *Growing Young: How Friendship, Optimism, and Kindness Can Help You Live to 100* that her studies found that people with healthy and supportive relationships live longer, and that these effects are surprisingly strong. Over the course of studies averaging seven years, results found that a committed romantic relationship lowers mortality by 49 percent, and a strong support network of family, friends, and neighbors lowers mortality risk by 45 percent. This is even more impressive when you consider that her research showed exercise only reduces mortality risk by 23 percent!

Furthermore, our relationships are 100 percent necessary to a significant life. It is through our close relationships as well as our connection to our broader community that we can realize our talents and live out our purpose. It is where we can find true meaning and fulfillment in our lives.

The family, friends, and neighbors that we call our village should be the most consistent and compassionate relationships in our life. These people provide authentic friendships based on trust and true candor. They challenge us and love us. But they are also the people we have fun with and enjoy the sweet moments of life with. These relationships make our lives better and our world more interesting.

FAMILY FIRST

The most important and often closest bonds we have in our lives are arguably those we find in our immediate family.

As we approach middle age, our family dynamics can be varied and full. Many of us are married or have life partners. Some of us are raising children and approaching life ahead as empty nesters. Some are married for a second time and dealing with multiple family units. Some are juggling it all within what is known as "the sandwich generation:" sandwiched between caring for our own children and, at the same time, beginning to care for our aging parents.

Regardless where we find ourselves with our family relationships, we are now at an age and place where we can decide how to strengthen and lean into all of these relationships in a way that will set us up for a more harmonious future.

Love and Marriage

We live in a time where there is a fluid view on the necessity of marriage, but for those who have chosen marriage or life partnership, this can be one of the most powerful and supportive relationships we can have in this life. At its best, it can be a beautiful bond where we find the most satisfaction and freedom to be ourselves. However, in today's individualistic society, we may miss the mark and assume marriage is an avenue to satisfy our needs, leaving the so-called partnership doomed to disappointment. Too often we expect that our spouse exists to make us happy—either by fulfilling our deepest longings or by making us look good. Those lofty expectations are too high for anyone to fulfill.

If we expect our spouse to love us unconditionally then we must offer the same in return.

> ***To be truly loved is to be truly known, and to be truly known means flaws and all.***

As bestselling author Marianne Williamson states, "Until we have seen someone's darkness we don't really know who they are. Until we have forgiven someone's darkness, we don't really know what love is."

Let's remember the work we have been doing on ourselves up to now. The deeper understanding of who you are and the ability to rest your identity in your purpose can take the pressure off of others in your life to be the ultimate source of happiness and fulfillment. If we suspend our ego drives and instead look at how we can grow and become better people within our marriages and families, the chances of survival are higher.

There is a biblical proverb that states "iron sharpens iron."[46] The idea that in our marriages we can sharpen each other into our best version of ourselves is a helpful framework to understanding the benefits of longevity within this key relationship. I must be open to receiving sharpening feedback from my spouse as much as, if not more than, being in pursuit to point out areas of improvement to him. When we realize that marriage is a sanctifying gift to help us be known and grow into a better version of ourselves, we are on the way to a long and healthy marriage led by love.

The Parent Trap

Parenting is one of the most beautiful gifts and opportunities you can be given in this world. It is also one of the hardest jobs on the planet. Oftentimes, we don't give it as much examination as we do our vocation, and as a result, we end up either overparenting or underparenting. We can be too present in the lives of our children, stunting their ability to advocate for themselves, or we can be physically or mentally absent in the small, daily moments, neglecting to nurture what matters most.

Our ultimate mission as parents is to teach our children how to spread their wings and fly so when they leave the nest they don't crash and burn. However, for people who have reached a certain level of success, it's hard not to view their children as agency to more achievement. A child who looks good, performs well, makes the winning shot, and attends the prestigious college is one more shiny accomplishment on the resume. Sadly, this often leads to overscheduled, exhausted, and anxious children.

I am not saying that we shouldn't hope our children succeed in life, only that we must not tie our children's success to our own. We must relieve the pressure valve, not increase it.

Famous British graffiti artist Banksy said, "Parents will do anything for their children except let them be themselves." We must allow our children to be who they are meant to be, fail when they need to fail, find their own passions, and discover their talents in their own time and way. We must see them and know them for who they are and then love them consistently regardless.

We are their guides, their mentors, and their protectors, but we do not do for them or go forth in their stead. While in our nest we must correct, instruct, and set proper boundaries. These boundaries give them a sense of safety and security. We are present not just physically but emotionally as well. But we also allow them to advocate for themselves, teaching them how to soar.

When we parent our children in a way that allows them to fly the nest on their own, we increase our chances of having a long life connected to them in a healthy relationship. We can realize our vision of a strong and connected family.

The Circle of Life

Watching our parents age is a strange and often difficult journey. Watching a parent die takes you to a place you can never prepare to go. Time grows more finite when engaging with our aging parents.

It's a tricky navigation for both parties. Our parents find it difficult to lose their freedom and have to rely on the children they worked hard to raise and release into the world. For people who have strained relationships with their parents, having to reengage in order to care for them often reopens old wounds. Suddenly, even though we are adults, we feel like angry little kids again. While lamenting that our parents haven't changed, we also may come to realize that we haven't done much growing yet either. Our interactions with them feel like a mirror is being held up to our eyes reflecting our own shortcomings.

Revisiting these relationships up close may come with the benefit of us using these final years with our parents to not only heal our bonds with them but evolve into a better human ourselves. Regardless of our relationship with our parents today, how we decide to live these final years with them rests with us.

At this stage of our lives, our worlds are vast and busy. Many of us are juggling big jobs and responsibilities at home with our own marriages and young children. We have many friends and community connections. For our senior-aged parents, most likely, their social circles have shrunk. Their responsibilities have diminished and many have nothing but time on their hands, while their human needs of safety, security, recognition, and love remain the same.

For most aging parents, their main source of fulfilling these essential needs comes from their adult children. Knowing this responsibility lies with you could sting if you still harbor the grief of a wounded childhood. It could also feel overwhelming if your plate already seems full. However, when we move toward a life of significance, we are able to more seamlessly prioritize and integrate the callings various seasons have on our life.

Try to optimize these relationships as best you can today. For those who have a secure and healthy relationship with their parents it may mean carving out time to be with them or talking to them on a regular basis. It may mean ensuring that your children have quality time with their grandparents.

For those whose relationship is fragile or fractured, it may mean being brave and working to heal past issues or hurts. You may need to make your feelings known while setting proper boundaries for a fresh start. If you have done your own work to grow as a person, that may be enough to break the childhood patterns and engage in a rewarding relationship with your parents moving forward.

These are precious years ahead that you won't get back. Decide how best to use them according to how healthy and secure your relationships are now and can become in the future.

THE FRIEND ZONE

Friends are the family we choose. Our chosen friends can be the most important support system we create for ourselves. But authentic, life-giving friendships do not come easily.

In 2017, the US Surgeon General called loneliness our greatest epidemic. The rise of technology increased our ability to connect while decreasing actual human contact. The COVID-19 pandemic introduced social distancing and isolation as well remote work into our societal patterns. We have not only a society artificially connected but one that may have forgotten how to properly engage each other.

Furthermore, today's criteria for friendship seem to have been diluted by the superficial sociability you find on Instagram, Facebook, or TikTok. Philosopher Alasdair MacIntyre writes, "Yet what above all else stands in the way of openness to friendship is insincerity... An insincere person invites others to respond not to their reality, but the sometimes impressive fiction that they have constructed." We cannot create the right village for ourselves based on an insincere, disconnected construct.

The type of friendship that makes a real difference to your life and the life of others is a small community of authentic connection. It is the type of friendship that is made over a cup of coffee or a walk around the block together. It is conversation that happens when we must look into each other's eyes and hear what the other person has to say.

Quality Not Quantity

As I considered the idea of an authentic community, I wondered: how many people am I supposed to be friends with?

British relationship mathematician and Oxford University evolutionary psychology professor Robin Dunbar says that human brains have a limit on how many meaningful relationships they can keep track of. His research shows that we should aim for around five intimate bonds (including spouse and close relatives), fifteen close friends (people we trust and spend time with regularly), fifty friends (people we might invite to an event), and 150 casual friendships (those acquaintances in our wider circle).

I think this framework is helpful in realizing that not only are our energy banks limited, so is our emotional capacity. Showing up consistently well for a large number of people is physically and mentally impossible. In a sense, social media may have incorrectly skewed our understanding of how many people truly are and should be our friends. The focus on social media is on the accumulation of friends, followers, and likes. A true community of friends is about quality, not mass quantity.

When we desire to be intentionally present and consistently available for our close friends, then we realize we must limit where and how we distribute our energy on a daily basis.

Our Most Trusted Advisors

Entrepreneur and author Jim Rohn famously said, "You are the average of the five people you spend the most time with." Rohn believes we are greatly influenced by those who immediately and most consistently surround us, and if we aren't intentional about who those people are, then we aren't setting ourselves up for a life of growth. For better or worse, our friends shape our thoughts, beliefs, and habits. Therefore, we shouldn't allow friendships to just happen to us. We should seek to grow and develop close friendships with those we know who add to our life, not subtract from it.

Oprah Winfrey refers to her small group of friends as her trusted advisors in life. She has nicknamed them her "Kitchen Cabinet." She says these are the people closest to her who will say, "What's wrong with you?" Being a revered celebrity, that candid accountability is something she knows she needs in her journey.

Business researcher and bestselling author Jim Collins calls his inner circle of wise friends a "Personal Council." Collins states, "Just as good entrepreneurs have strong boards for their companies, you should also have a strong board of directors for your life. These are the people who are like a tribal-elders council of people whom you can turn to for guidance, input, and wisdom. And they're also people whom you would feel terrible to let down."

Creating this type of tribal-elders council in our personal life takes a certain level of intentionality and selectivity to create a long-lasting, intimate group of confidants. We must look mindfully at those we hold closest to us.

Aristotle believed that perfect friendship only happened between two people who were both models of goodness and virtue and had a "mutual concern of each person for the other for his own sake." In other words, friendships based on mutual values and concern for each other had the strongest effect on our lives and greatest chance for survival. Our closest confidants should be people who share our values or have true concern for our well-being if we expect them to last a lifetime.

Our closest advisors in our life can and should serve as a source of clarity and truth especially when we are at a crossroads. Because of a solid foundation of trust, it is with these friends that you can share the most brutal facts about any situation. Our friends don't shame us, but they do hold us accountable. They are honest with us so we can be honest with them. We expect and can receive impartial feedback from them. Your dearest friends don't pacify or placate. Because they want the very best for you, they are candid and curious. They will help you dissect and diagnose.

Don't Go It Alone

Many successful people know the importance of wise and seasoned leaders or mentors in the workplace but may not recognize the need for tribal-elders in their everyday personal life. It is not uncommon for me to have a successful entrepreneur client who does not have many, if any, close friends.

In my experience this tends to show up more often with my male clients. Some are happy to only have the ear of their spouse or life partner. Some rely on their business partner or a colleague at work to casually bounce off an idea or issue. While those relationships are important, I push them to consider broadening their circle of confidants.

It's easy to get caught up in leading a business or navigating various responsibilities and then not realize what issues or problems we may be missing. We start to make decisions in a vacuum. It's hard to see the forest for the trees when you don't have a wider council of people giving you honest evaluation or advice. We should not fear constructive criticism. If you seek out wise, mature, and trusted confidants, then the feedback you receive will indeed make your life better.

We should strive for those ideal friendships in our lives and nothing less. Our time and energy are precious, and we should walk through the passages of life and death with real friends by our side.

My good friends have been instrumental in pushing me in ways I never would have on my own. They also believe in me in ways that are different even from my husband. I have friends who don't just support my happiness but long for it. In return, I want to be there for them as well. My wise council of trusted advisors has been by my side for many years, and I hope they will be there until the end. I have no intention of ever flying solo.

As William Shakespeare said, "A friend is one that knows you as you are, understands where you have been, accepts what you have become, and still, gently allows you to grow."

A Committed Friend

The greatest danger to our individual friendships and collective authentic community is withheld love and compassion. We are either conduits to love or we are not. We are either leaning into connecting with others or we consciously or subconsciously disconnect or divide.

Self-awareness of how we show up in our friendships will help us understand which category we fall into and if we need to course correct. Only you can decide if, when, and how to show up. The choice on how to connect rests with us.

When we approach our friends with curiosity, we learn to walk in their shoes and hear their stories. We then show up for our friends with empathy in a way they truly need us. We don't rush in to always fix but we seek first to understand.

C.S. Lewis said, "Friendship is born at that moment when one person says to another, 'What! You too? I thought I was the only one.'" There is beauty in sharing your story and hearing someone else say, "me too." It is that connection that reminds us we aren't walking this journey alone.

Commit to those in your life who are willing and able to make that same commitment to you. Pour into those relationships and show up well. You will see your friendships blossom and grow.

SHARED ROOTS OF COMMUNITY

As we look to cultivate deeper roots in our relationships, the Pando is a life-giving metaphor to consider. The Pando is an immense grove of aspen trees in Utah that happens to be the largest organism in the world. Why would a grove be considered one organism? Above ground it appears as a forest of trees, but below ground it shares one singular root system.

When given the space and conditions to flourish, the Pando reproduces rapidly across neighboring valleys. This reminds me of our society when it is at its best. One large organism, sharing resources and space, multiplying yet connected at its core. It is a beautiful idea of what our world could be or rather should be. A village, connected at the heart and soul.

Unfortunately, the Pando is in danger. After thousands of years, it is dying. Grazing cattle feeding on its young offshoots and urban development in the area are two major threats to its existence. The groves have shrunk in size and thinned out. Pando are surviving only in the protected areas in Utah.

Could this be a metaphor for what is happening in our culture today? Has our growth as a connected and unified community been splintered and fractured? Or does it just appear this way on the surface and in the media? Can we create an authentic village for ourselves while trying to unify the world toward the greater good? Is it worth the effort?

Divided We Fall

As I write this chapter, the United States is extremely divided. Rather than seeking out compassionate community or vulnerability-based friendships, people are flocking to a toxic form of tribalism, finding their purpose in cultlike followings that preach extreme exclusion and foster societal division and only finding justice in *their* way of believing and doing. The extreme tribes work hard to discredit, disavow, and simply hate the alternative tribe. It is a cold war that feels red hot.

> *"We divide easily because we love shallowly."*
>
> **—FRANCIS CHAN**

Though many of the leaders behind these tribes offer a rallying cry for the masses of frustrated citizens, the vitriol at the center of their call has eroded the soul and connective tissue of our culture today. We are a fractured people that seems adrift. We are untethered. Individualism, personal freedom, and materialism are currently winning the game of life, but it doesn't have to be that way—and it can't be sustained much longer.

We can find hope when we realize that toxic tribalism is as old as your seventh-grade lunch table. We've been drawn to group identities to find a sense of belonging since the beginning of time. But it's impossible to create the authentic community we are looking for when the world is made up of little islands rather than being woven together as part of one society for the greater good.

We must work hard to bridge the gap and make a difference where we are today. We must identify and call out toxic tribalism for what it is: groups joined together through hate, spite, or jealousy. Then, we must promote the opposite. We must focus on building our villages based on love.

When Jesus Christ was asked what he believed the greatest commandment to be, He said, "Love the Lord your God with all your heart and with all your soul and with all your mind. This is the first and greatest commandment. And the second is like it: 'Love your neighbor as yourself.'"[47]

That's it. Love God. Love your neighbor.

Who's your neighbor? Everyone.

Loving everyone is not a complex idea, but it is hard to execute. It may sometimes feel like swimming upstream. This kind of inclusive love often takes us way beyond our comfort zone and can be challenging to achieve because the insecurities and narcissism of our ego get in the way. It is only when we realize that we long to be loved as well that we can let go of ego and love those around us.

Author, professor, and researcher Dr. Karen Swallow Prior writes, "The age of the autonomous individual, the age of the narcissistic self, the age of consumerism and moral drift has left us with bitterness and division, a surging mental health crisis and people just being nasty to one another. Millions are looking for something else, some system of belief that is communal, that gives life transcendent meaning."

The hope is that through our commitment to a significant life we can provide something new and different that will bring meaning through community. We must first recognize that we have much more in common than what we see on the divisive surface. There is more to a book than its cover.

All Together Now

After twenty-five years living in the city of Chicago, my family decided to make a big move to Nashville, Tennessee. This seemed unreal to our family and friends. I've always been a big-city girl. I love Chicago. I immediately fell in love with the energy and unexpectedness of the city. I remember seeing a cab driver in a screaming match with a messenger on a bicycle in the middle of downtown Chicago. This wasn't an unusual scene in the pre-internet nineties to see bicycle messengers regularly cutting in and out of traffic with near misses of the hundreds of cabs that ruled the streets. Amid the screaming, I turned to my friend and said, "Man, I love this city." To me, this unabashed chaos was the fuel to my big-city dreams.

But as we aged and our children grew, our needs and desires shifted. We decided it was time to leave all we knew and embark on a new adventure. After a road trip visiting various cities, we fell in love with the beauty and friendliness of Nashville. There were just enough big-city transplants to make us feel at home while space for us to stretch our legs.

One of the biggest adjustments was an unexpected one. In Chicago, our neighbors were close. Literally. If I had my windows open at home, I could hear my neighbor sneeze. We had over sixty kids on our one city block. Kids would pop from house to house with ease. We walked everywhere and rarely drove more than a few miles a day. Yes, the city was crowded, somewhat dirty, and sometimes dangerous, but the community was real. I saw and spoke to my neighbors on a daily basis.

We settled into a bigger home in the South—where you do indeed get more for your money. More space means I don't hear my neighbor sneeze. I don't hear much of anything. If I woke up in the middle of the night in Chicago, I could often hear the Irving Park Road bus open its door and announce its stop. Here I hear the sound of a cricket or two.

Community isn't worse or better; it's just different. Our neighborhood women, in Southern fashion, host monthly luncheons, and we each bring something for the potluck. The kids take turns at each other's houses to swim or watch movie marathons. We aren't walking everywhere, but we have created a new village that operates differently.

Looking across the two very different living experiences, I have come to realize that community may look different in various parts of the country, but it is available should you desire and seek it out.

All this change has made me think about what really defines a community. Your community is your social unit. It is who you fellowship with and do life with outside of your family. It is your friends, your neighbors, and those in your town or city. It is those who you seek out that share your same values, attitudes, and goals in life. It's those you share a common unity with.

Your community will look different depending on where you live and what stage of life you are in. During some stages, it will feel easier to form a community. In other stages you may feel more isolated. Moves or shifts can also alter your sense of community. Regardless, one thing is for certain: community takes effort.

I believe everyone should move at least once in their adult life, if possible. For me, it was an enlightening gift, taking me off autopilot and reengaging me in life. After we moved to Nashville, I found that trying to make new friends at my age was surprisingly scary and somewhat exhausting. The idea of starting over was daunting, but I knew that I'd regret, maybe even resent, the move if I didn't get out there and say hello. It didn't take long to form great relationships with good people. Being in a different city with a new culture and climate was invigorating and inspiring. Starting over isn't easy, but sometimes it's worth shaking up your world to bring yourself into greater awareness of who you are and what you want. It will also help you to see that we have so much more in common than you can imagine.

I moved across the country, crossing the Mason-Dixon Line, and surprisingly have found that on the surface, America may seem very different, but face-to-face we are so very much the same. We do belong to a tribe. The human race. Once we commit to that one tribe and point others in that same direction, we will be one step closer to the unity we so desperately desire.

JOY IN THE SIGNIFICANT

Even though we have just examined our life through the lens of our relationship with ourselves and with others, we need to resist the urge to live in a compartmentalized way. To avoid getting tripped up on the idea that we have to equally divide our time across each area or person in our life, we need to keep the goal of moving organically and seamlessly through all the priorities of our life.

The best companies we work with are those who understand that certain departments will need more attention than others given phases or trajectories of the business. They also understand that departments must work together as one unit and avoid becoming siloed or disconnected from other areas. The same is true for our lives.

We can and should show up well, living our purpose intentionally within ourselves and with all we encounter. We must look at our lives as one integrated experience. It is our story, and we are the hero on a journey engaging with our talents and passions and positively impacting the other characters.

It's no surprise that the people who seamlessly integrate all their priorities in a healthful and balanced way tend to be the people we find most joyful. These are the minority, who have recognized all the components of their life and haven't given up one in exchange for another. They do not have a thriving career yet little connection to their family. They do not pour their entire life into their children and then have no space to give to the community around them. They do not solely focus on their own health at the expense of their business endeavors. Instead, they live holistically, intentionally caring for the health and well-being of themselves and their community.

These are people who have found proper balance because they understand when and how to show up. They are calm due to the focused and loving commitment they have made to themselves and to those important in their lives. They have found balance by eliminating the unnecessary and showing up well to the essential aspects of their life. They have found the ultimate freedom in letting go of their ego and fearlessly saying no to commitments and people who do not support their purpose.

It is not that these joyful people do not experience sadness or grief. Rather, they are the ones who are able to feel those emotions most deeply and in turn reap the benefits of more wisdom for the journey ahead. They are not complacent in their living and therefore they have the space and energy to feel all that they are experiencing and then grow and transform because of it. They are unstuck. They have found themselves and yet given themselves away; through it all they have found a more whole way of living. A life committed to one of significance.

THE POWER OF A VILLAGE

In her groundbreaking book *Braving the Wilderness*, Brené Brown tells the story of a small village where women would come together by a river to wash their clothes. Beyond just a time for a weekly chore, it was here that the women would commune and share the highs and lows of everyday life with each other week after week.

Then one day the future arrived in the form of washing machines, and no longer was there a need to meet at the river for the taxing chore of hand-washing clothes. One might assume that would be cause for celebration; however, not long after the households in the village were introduced to washing machines, there was an outbreak of depression. While a little more wealth and technology may have brought physical relief, the disappearance of gathering weekly with the community had a profound effect on the mental health of the village.

We live in a country where washing machines, dishwashers, and private backyards can lead to feeling like we are alone on a deserted island. Many of us can go an entire day without human interaction if we so desire. But we weren't created for such a solitary existence. We can believe that our computers and phones are enough to keep us connected, but in the end they are not giving us the depth of relationship that our soul truly needs.

One of the many gifts that a village gives us is the ability to belong and therefore know our worth. A strong sense of belonging leads to a strong sense of worthiness. Brown highlights her research in the book on what it means to truly belong in an age of increased polarization, stating that "the people who have a strong sense of love and belonging believe that they are worthy of love and belonging—that's it."

An individualistic, self-serving, and isolated society is not working. It is wreaking havoc on our physical, mental, intellectual, and spiritual health. Our growth will remain stunted until we move toward building and expanding an authentic village. We are social creatures who thrive on human connection. Belonging is found when we each commit to a life of significant relationships.

We can have our modern washing machines, but we must work to ensure we have the village by the river, too. It is there where we can find rest in the life-giving connection of fellow humans. Within a village, we experience belonging. With belonging, we realize our true worth. That's the power of a village.

Reflections

- Take some time to outline your Village. What family members and friends are in your village, and how are each of the relationships?
- Do you have a trusted group of advisors?
- How do you engage your community?
- Outline some steps you need to take to strengthen and fortify your village.

CHAPTER NINE

YOUR WORK

"Don't judge each day by the harvest you reap but by the seeds that you plant."

—ROBERT LOUIS STEVENSON

One of my favorite movies is the 1946 classic *It's a Wonderful Life.* It is considered one of the greatest films of all time, and watching it is a Christmas tradition in my house.

Clarence, a second-class angel who is working diligently to earn his wings, is sent from heaven after hearing the prayers for a man named George Bailey. George is a desperately frustrated businessman who is toying with the idea of ending it all.

After the death of his father, George's early dreams—to leave his small town, travel the world, and find fame and fortune—become compromised as he instead takes over the family business. As time marches on, hardship continues to show up at his door. He spends his entire life giving up his big dreams for the good of his town, Bedford Falls.

One Christmas Eve, a financial discrepancy puts George in a difficult position. Despite being adored by his family and revered by the hardworking people of Bedford Falls, George believes he's worth more dead than alive and is ready to take his own life. That's when Clarence appears and strives to show him what life would have been like if he had never been born. In this alternate, George-less universe, he discovers how much he and his work meant to so many people. George begs for his life back—and suddenly, the real world returns.

Maybe this movie is so beloved after all these years because it is extremely relatable. Without seeing the deeper meaning in our work, we are bound to find ourselves exhausted, overwhelmed, and desperate. Often, in all the noise of the whirlwind of our lives, the only thing we're left to hear is the ringing question "what is this all for?"

When we struggle to see why our work matters, we end up feeling trapped, unfulfilled, and confused, even if we are exactly in the job we should be. Because it's unlikely Clarence will be swooping in to illuminate the worth we bring to each of our lives, this chapter is designed to help you identify deeper meaning in one of your largest Life Zones: your work.

Finding purpose and meaning in your work should be a priority. Most of us naturally desire this. We want our work to matter. For some of us that means rekindling the flame. For others, it may mean starting fresh. We will use the pages ahead to explore three ways to breathe new life and significance back into your work:

1) Finding the Renewed Motivation to Work
2) Finding Real Fulfillment in Work
3) Finding the Right Place to Work

FINDING THE RENEWED MOTIVATION TO WORK

> *"Ever more people today have the means to live, but no meaning to live for."*
>
> **—VIKTOR E. FRANKL**

We can all be like George Bailey, not fully appreciating what we have or dwelling on the unrealized dreams of our life. I know I was. Without realizing it, we can become entirely consumed by never-ending stresses and lose ourselves in dread or drudgery. When we cannot find meaning in the moments of our day, we can lose our motivation—maybe not to live, like George, but to work.

I had lost the will to work during my final years at HGTV. Previously, my motivation to climb the corporate ladder was enough to get me to leap out of bed each morning and pay my dues. Now that I was standing at the top of the ladder, that once-familiar motivation had waned. Suddenly my new lack of drive was causing questions to arise. Going through the predetermined mile markers had worked well, but now I was at a standstill.

Even though I liked my job and felt I was very good at it, I was struggling to put it into the greater context of my life. I was in a vacuum trying to find meaning for myself in a career I had never previously questioned. But it wasn't just the questions that left me empty. It was my limited understanding of the idea of "work." Working simply for the money and to pad my identity was not satisfying. I needed a bigger tool kit to navigate the expansive inner work that lay before me. I needed a renewed motivation.

Consumption and Identity

It's common to get caught up in a "work-for-consumption" mindset that views work as simply a means to subsidize the lifestyle we desire. When we work for consumption, without a deeper motivation, we are more likely to view our work as transactional toil. We work and get paid in return. In some regards, this simplistic mindset is easy to maintain because it puts little pressure on the worker to consider their job in a greater context. Just show up and do the job, and you'll get compensated.

On the flip side, this exchange can steer us to endure work without real meaning. The discomfort we feel when doubting if our work really matters can lead us to avoidance or escapism. In turn, we focus on finding relief, comfort, and a more luxurious lifestyle. Work becomes a necessary evil to give us the things we most desire and ease the pain of Monday through Friday. We work for the weekend or to get to the next vacation, but the only destination we ever reach is an island of burnout and despair.

Alongside consuming goods, our ego is hungry too, and with consumption as the motivator, we can tend to view our work as a means to personal achievement and status. Put simply, work becomes a channel to consume and an avenue to achieve.

As previously examined, it is important not to wrap our identity in any one part of our life. However, because our society places a great emphasis on finding our fullness in our vocational success, we may continually wrestle most with untangling our identity from our work.

Unchecked success can go straight to our heads, leading to a puffed-up, unapproachable version of ourselves. Unchecked failure can crush us to the point of complete despair, completely disrupting the peace in other areas of our lives. Either way, we have lost ourselves by allowing our entire self-worth to be dependent on our vocation.

This work-centric identity especially traps those without active employment. If you are laid off from work, you are left stripped of your identity and deemed unnecessary or no longer vital. If you are a stay-at-home parent, you feel undervalued because society has placed its highest esteem upon those with power and paychecks.

Too often we can mistakenly call our roles in life our calling or true identity. I'm a doctor, a lawyer, a writer, an artist, a mom, a dad, a homemaker, a teacher, a police officer—these titles or roles become the sum of who we think we are rather than simply one key responsibility we have in our life. It's true that these roles are big parts of our lives and that we should celebrate our achievements, but these titles do not equal the sum of us.

Many are hanging on to a job only because giving up the title will leave them feeling naked. Even if you've found outward success in your roles, keep in mind that without knowing your greater purpose, your title or the prestige of the company will never outweigh the miserable, long days of a meaningless existence within it.

It's time to end the wrestling match with consuming and achieving and free ourselves from the handcuffs of a work-based identity.

The Real Why of Work

> *"Let's start at the very beginning, a very good place to start."*
>
> **—FRAULEIN MARIA, THE SOUND OF MUSIC**

Work makes the best sense to us when placed in a bigger picture. It helps to take a deep breath and see that we are part of something greater and, therefore, contributing to an ongoing and ever-evolving creation. To find a renewed motivation for work, we need to understand the tangled roots of our present-day Western workplace experience.

Historically, the biggest "why" for work has been subsistence. We worked to survive. We needed food, water, shelter, and clothing. We hunted, gathered, and built. We then traded and competed, creating classes of workers and divisions of labor. During the Renaissance, we began to be rewarded for our genius and creativity. During the Reformation, we were introduced to the idea of a work ethic and finding dignity in "good and moral" work. As society grew and technology evolved, the creation of factories and mass production took hold. The business world grew into corporate America.

With each innovation, we continually became disconnected from personal meaning in our work, and for many, they were left feeling like a cog in the wheel.

Today we sit at a crossroads. Disengagement feels almost like an epidemic. Gallup states, "For the first year in more than a decade, the percentage of engaged workers in the US declined in 2021. Just over one-third of employees (34 percent) were engaged." This means that roughly two-thirds of us are just showing up.

To their credit, the millennial generation, motivated by finding deeper personal fulfillment and helping the greater good, has given a louder voice to an examination of why we work. Post-pandemic, most of us, regardless of age, find that work is no longer an exact location with set working hours. Given this lapse in space and time, we are left to muster up the motivation to keep moving forward.

Work for Contribution

> *"The one who plants trees, knowing that he will never sit in their shade, has at least started to understand the meaning of life."*
>
> **—RABINDRANATH TAGORE**

Before we race into the future of work, we need to go back to the beginning to find a better way.

One of the earliest recorded mentions of work is in the book of Genesis, the very first book of the Bible or the Jewish Torah. God works for six days to create the earth and then on the seventh day, after declaring His work "good," he rests. He instructed the humans he created on earth to "work and keep it." It's clear from the beginning that contribution is part of our purpose as humans.

We are designed to cultivate and maintain. We are free to declare our work good. We are free to reward ourselves with rest. This original teaching on work gives us not only clear direction from the start but a healthy perspective for the future. Even though work is labor, it is not a bad thing that must be endured or whose sole purpose is to sustain us economically. It can be hard, but it is ultimately good and was designed for a purpose.

The contribution mindset as described in these sacred beliefs is one that pulls us beyond our base needs or desires and pushes us outside ourselves. It is in our contribution to the cultivation and betterment of our society where we can find meaning. This can be found in the tasks or craft of our work but also in the connection it gives us to other humans and to society at large. We can also find individual satisfaction and fulfillment in the idea that our work can and should be good.

We begin to see work as no longer an individual experience but more as a collective. When we make contribution—rather than consumption—our goal, the path to cultivating more for the world, impacting others, and living out our purpose naturally becomes a road more easily traveled.

Looking at work as an avenue to opportunity for meaningful contribution creates a new kind of power in your life. Amy Wrzesniewski, a professor at Yale and formulator of a practice called *job crafting*, conducted an in-depth survey of hospital custodial workers.[48] She found that some defined their job as cleaning the floor and others as creating a safe place for patients. One worker even went so far as to say, "I'm a healer. I create sterile spaces in the hospital. My role here is to do everything I can to promote the healing of the patients." It's this attitude of service that has allowed some workers to find heightened happiness in their work and see the meaning in a job well done.

Similarly, my clients who find the most satisfaction in their work tend to be those who learn to see the dignity in what they do every day and can call it out in others as well. Rather than counting down the days to retirement, this perspective causes them to think they may never have enough days or years to impact the world.

When we understand that we were designed for good work and the honor that surrounds the impact we make, regardless of our status, title, or paycheck, our eyes are open to the noble pursuit of contribution to our society.

Having this renewed motivation to work enables us to build a life we truly want. Work is such a large part of our journey, and understanding its meaning sets the stage for finding fulfillment where we are, no matter what stage of our career.

FINDING REAL FULFILLMENT IN WORK

When it comes to curing the disengagement epidemic, it appears that finding purpose at work is the key.[49]

When your point of view is shaped by living out your purpose in the workplace rather than searching for your identity there, your work doesn't own you. Instead, you own it. It doesn't rest in that slow march of meaningless boredom nor in the wild ride of ill-placed identity. Instead, it can become significant.

Various social scientists, organizational psychologists, business leaders, and authors have come to the same conclusion about human motivation and work. Ultimately, we are driven by our innate human needs for achieving one's full potential, esteem, and belonging. When these core needs are met, we find ourselves not only satisfied but enjoying our work.

My own personal findings align with these views. I find that my clients are most fulfilled when they have found three key factors in their work: ***Mastery***, ***Agency***, and ***Connection***. Once they have satisfied all three of these needs, they appear more satisfied and purposeful in their vocations. They begin to look more intently for ways to have maximum impact in the world around them.

Work For Mastery

Excellence at your work requires commitment to mastery of your craft or service. A commitment to mastery makes you a lifelong learner. The mountaineer W.H. Murray once said, "Until one is committed, there is hesitancy." It's a powerful realization to know that once you commit to mastery, there is no end to the journey. Your goal becomes progress in your abilities each day.

> *"We don't make movies to make money. We make movies to make money so we can make better movies."*
>
> **—WALT DISNEY**

One of my favorite documentaries is called *Jiro Dreams of Sushi*. It follows a famous Japanese chef, Jiro Ono, who has run a sushi restaurant under a subway station in Tokyo for over fifty years. There is no menu. He makes each guest twenty pieces of sushi. Jiro has devoted his entire life to the mastery of his craft. One of the most memorable moments in the film is when it is time to prepare octopus. Jiro demands the octopus be massaged for thirty minutes to ensure complete tenderness. After watching the film, you almost can't order octopus at your local sushi restaurant anymore. You know it just won't be tender enough. Jiro is a master who strives for excellence. He is dedicated to quality, not quantity.

He has found joy in his work in one of the most unlikely spaces —a tiny slip of a restaurant in an unattractive, underground hallway. It does not matter to him. He is fulfilled by the enterprise to master his craft, believing that the journey has no end. He will always be learning and growing; becoming better with each piece of sushi.

Ikigai is a Japanese word used to describe one's purpose and meaning of life. The word literally consists of *iki* (to live) and *gai* (reason). I believe Jiro has found his reason to live. As I write this, he is alive and well and ninety-six years old. Maybe his long life could in part be attributed to his dedication to mastering his craft.

> *"I'll keep climbing, trying to reach the top, but nobody knows where the top is."*
>
> —JIRO

Aiming for continual progress rather than unattainable perfection sets us on the right course to find satisfaction in our daily pursuits. Progress toward mastery becomes a healthy desire that can be exciting in our lives and makes us more productive, dedicated, and fulfilled in our work.

Work with Agency

I remember visiting my daughters at their Montessori elementary school when they were younger. Montessori school founder Maria Montessori believed in self-directed working in the classroom and that it cultivated a love of learning. I marveled as I watched my children take out their daily task list and decide with great thought what they'd like to do first. Knowing that they needed to complete the list by the end of the day, I was able to see how my daughters and their classmates, despite their young ages, prioritized and worked. They felt in control and rather proud to show me their best routine and dedication to complete the day. A doubter of the process at first, I became a champion for the Montessori philosophy. I saw how agency and autonomy created discipline and productivity.

In a 2010 study released in the *Journal of Management*, researchers found that millennials valued more freedom and autonomy at work than previous generations. Unlike Generation X and baby boomers, millennials were found to desire leisure time over status and money. This shift has continued to build for the overall workforce over this last decade. Now the drive to control our own destiny and shape our lives is feeding into our short- and long-term demands at work.

In the short term, younger generations are seeking out flexibility, diminished commute times, and freedom to switch companies when growth opportunities dry up. For older generations, working on your own terms means deciding how hard and how much you are going to work in the remaining years ahead.

Post-pandemic, there is a different discussion about autonomy. The freedom and self-direction that many were longing for was dropped in our laps with new work-from-home protocols. Now, no one is watching, and we have largely been left to decide the day.

If you have reached a certain level of success or have worked at a place long enough, you have probably earned some well-deserved autonomy. You can control your schedule more than you were able when you were first starting out. You can allow yourself certain freedoms that were not available when you were "earning your stripes." Having some flexibility and control over how we work is a very fulfilling element in a vocation. It is one that we should not only look for but treasure as we think about the future.

This can be a difficult concept for those who have been on the high-speed success train. It's hard to let go and place more responsibility in the hands of your employees or not feel guilty that you aren't connected to your team 24/7. Hopefully at this stage of your career the time you give to your work is high-quality and not high-quantity driven. Your future should include living out your purpose and passions by your own design.

Once you have let go of your identity being rooted in others' opinions or society's measure of success, you can find more mental freedom as well. You can wake up and decide what to do without the trappings of the golden handcuffs and regime of ladder climbing. It may take a new level of confidence and risk, but you've earned the right to explore new horizons.

I attribute the growing desire I had for more agency as one of the key reasons I decided to leave HGTV. After almost two decades in a large media corporation, I was eager for more freedom to decide for myself how and when I wanted to work. Being an executive with immense responsibility means needing to be available at any given moment. For some, that demanding schedule provides security or excitement, but for me, I was ready to let go of those demands to design a workweek that better suited my stage in life. I was also ready to embark on new entrepreneurial endeavors. Leaving my big corporate job meant climbing back into the driver's seat.

Work for Connection

Famous writer and poet Kahlil Gibran once said, "Work is love made visible." You can love what you do, love who you do it with, or love who you do it for. You can make love visible in so many different ways through your work.

To belong and be loved is a basic human need. The opportunity to realize this need and connect through our work is there almost every day if we slow down to notice. It can be found in the way you connect the dots for someone, how you bring an idea to life, or seeing the smile on a customer's face.

We all can become dissatisfied too easily or bored too quickly, or think the grass is always greener on the other side. Too often we want a job that's a little more exciting, with a little more pay, a little more power, and a little more recognition. This can happen when we lose sight of how to best connect to those around us. How can we touch their lives? How can we have a positive impact even on the days when work is hard, boring, or repetitive? How can we see our small moments of connection as big steps toward significance?

Sometimes I will be working with a client who is constantly trying to figure out why things aren't going well at work, why they are unsatisfied and unhappy, and why they aren't achieving their goals. They try to pin it on the people they work with or the company itself, but when pressed, they find it difficult to give specific examples or clearly articulate a problem. Suddenly, the aha moment hits. Maybe the problem is them.

> ***Often, when we are serving only ourselves on the road to success, we become our main problem.***

When we shift focus from ourselves and our ultimate success and start looking at how we can benefit and support others, we can create a more fruitful work experience. We can equip and train those around us, multiply our impact, and spread the rewards.

As I grew as a leader at HGTV, I began to see what others needed from me. My staff needed me to be available, competent, fair, and open. They needed me to connect. That connection was a sign that I valued them. I found that my staff was more curious about how much I truly cared than how much I knew. When I showed that I cared about their future, their growth, and their happiness, they worked harder and smarter. I allowed space for fun and laughter. The more I leaned in, the more they were able to shine and enjoy work. In turn, I was able to have a lot of fun too! You've likely heard the truism, "You can't change others, but you can change yourself." Turns out changing yourself leads to others changing themselves for the better too.

It's hard to see television or advertising as a worthy cause or higher calling. That may be true for your industry as well. But when we see our place among a group of people, we can make our work experience mean something, and that can lead to the company as a whole living out its core values more clearly and therefore impacting the world in a better way. I believe the leaders of HGTV realized their opportunity was beyond just getting advertisers to invest in their programming. HGTV realized its opportunity to bring something more to the world through its commitment to the people who worked there. They were creating an environment where inspiration and connection happened for the people in their offices, edit rooms, and shoots—and in turn, their viewers at home.

Try to realize in your work that there is hope for the better. A better you. A better team. Maybe even a better world. Do not lose faith; remain focused on your purpose. You may never know all the seeds you plant. You may not live long enough to see everything you do blossom into reality. That's okay. You are leaving behind a greater legacy by leaning into the meaning of your work.

FINDING THE RIGHT PLACE TO WORK

We have all experienced it: a time in our career when we have sat at our desk and wondered, "should I stay or should I go?" You wrestle between the current comfort of staying put against the unknown possibilities on the horizon.

Maybe something has awoken you to consider a departure. Perhaps it is a desire to advance or start a new venture. You know in the past you've thrived on the excitement of a new experience and think maybe you just need a change. Or perhaps you are struggling with an unhealthy culture or a conflict-ridden relationship with a business partner or colleague and just need a break and some fresh air again.

Changing career paths, especially toward midlife, is not a decision that can be taken lightly. Whether you thrive on change and are ready to shake things up or feel paralyzed by the idea of leaving the relative safety and security of your current situation, weighing your next best move requires intentional time and thought.

A Working Compass

To move into a life we actually want, we must continually hold our work up to the Life Compass that guides us. As we discovered in Chapter Six, our Life Compass consists of our unique talents, current passions, personal core values, and core purpose statement. When used as a filter to our work, we can ascertain what company, organization, or role is right for us and whether or not our current position still fits who we have become. This compass lets us know if we are headed in the right direction or if it is time to course correct.

Being in a job or at a company that doesn't align with who we are is like being lost on a journey. You end up somewhere unintended, and the days become very uncomfortable. It could be that the role requires a skillset we do not possess. It could be that no matter how hard we try, we feel no passion, spark, or love for what we are doing. We could find that the company's purpose is vastly different from our own. We could be in an environment that exhibits behaviors that do not align with our values, and we find each day to be at odds with our deepest beliefs.

When our work lacks synergy with who we are, it will be very difficult to find any joy in what we are doing each day. It is important to note that there are no perfect jobs. But with awareness and intention you can find the right place to work and foster a career that brings you joy.

Can You Make It Work?

Many of my clients mistakenly believe that a new job will be a silver bullet to happiness or a good life. Work should not make us miserable or suck us dry, but as we've been landing on throughout this book, it is not the key to ultimate happiness.

When weighing whether a client should stay in their current role or move on, I always start by asking, "Is the existing workplace situation changeable? Can you remedy the difficult relationship with your business partner? Can you create a new position that will provide you with the challenge you are craving? Can you change your job description to better suit your purpose and talents?"

Your first step should always be to try and make it work where you are now. In our success-driven, fast-paced world, we can make emotionally charged snap decisions that don't permanently solve the problem. These abrupt decisions often put us in a different place with the same concerns, especially if the issues are due to our own limitations. We must take the time to unpack whether the difficulties we are dealing with can be remedied first before jumping ship. Take a breath and lay out your options. Seek wise counsel and honest feedback. It may require effort, confrontation, or courage to fix your current situation, but it could be well worth it in the long run.

At its core, work should be a healthy avenue to live out your talents and purpose. If you cannot find an opportunity to do that where you currently are, then it may be time to say goodbye. If this is your situation, my best advice is to leave well. When you decide to move on, you want to confidently be able to look in the rearview mirror and say you did your best. Many regrets result from burned bridges. Give your utmost while you remain in your current role and hope for the best when you are on the way out. Do not poison the well as you exit. Save your constructive criticism for your exit interview, not the proverbial watercooler. Be grateful for the experience you had even if it wasn't ideal. There is no better feeling than knowing you are leaving a place better than you found it and, for some, knowing the door is always open should you one day wish to return.

Putting Your Dreams to Work

Many people who reach out to me have a secret desire or dream job they have fantasized about for many years. It may have been the thing they said they wanted to be when they grew up. At age seven, I firmly believed I belonged on stage, and whenever anyone asked me what I wanted to be when I grew up, I confidently replied, "an actress and singer!"

As we age, many of those dreams get discarded. But once we reach our middle-age years, our old dreams have a way of evolving into new visions and hopes. Maybe it's opening up a bakery or designing our own clothes. It could be becoming a golf instructor or owning a tutoring business. You may long to design new software or create a not-for-profit for a cause close to your heart. While some day-dreams align with our hopes as a child, others can be newly inspired by a more recent life experience. No matter how it came to be, it's a gift to your future to put your dream to the test.

Vetting the Dream

The first step I take with my clients is to have them tell me the story of their dream. How did it come to be? When were they first inspired?

How often does it pop into their head? Hearing the origin story of their dream helps me understand if they see their dream clearly and how firmly it belongs to them.

Next, we look at their dream against their Life Compass. Does it align with how they have been uniquely designed? Do they have the ability to be successful at it? Will it be a true vocation, paid work that can sustain them?

Sometimes people have a passion or love for something but do not have the right talents to excel at it. I see this with successful people, who feel if they've greatly succeeded at one thing then they can find success again through sheer determination alone. Jim Collins talks about this idea when working with companies in his bestselling book *Good to Great*. He describes what he calls the *Hedgehog Concept*. He believes great companies evaluate their ideas through the lens of three criteria: 1) what you are deeply passionate about; 2) what you can be the best in the world at; and 3) what best drives your economic or resource engine.[50]

Collins writes, "Every company would like to be the best at something, but few actually understand—with piercing insight and egoless clarity—what they actually have the potential to be the best at and, just as important, what they cannot be the best at."

Being honest with yourself about what you are best at and passionate about and what will drive your economic engine will help keep you from getting stuck on a dream with which you ultimately have no chance of excelling. While I may not find financial success as an actress or a singer at this point in my life, my fearless desire to be on stage or entertain an audience is a dream I can realize through my various speaking engagements. The innate drive to hop on a stage that I have had since a young age, along with my natural speaking talents, has financially served me very well over the years.

If the dream matches up to your personal Hedgehog Concept, then look at what it would take to execute it. Do you need training or to go back to school? How much money is required? Would your family support the dream? Could you begin to pursue the dream while maintaining your current vocational situation or job? In other words, are you willing to risk the cost to pursue it?

If it doesn't align, then you may want to consider playing out a version of your dream as a hobby or volunteer opportunity but not base an entire career change on it. Remember to evaluate if your dream can become a viable economic engine to financially support your life. Sometimes you need to wait to launch your idea when you have proper funding or the market conditions are better. It most likely will not be financially feasible if it is incongruent with your gifting and purpose. It is extremely hard to find financial success with something you aren't innately talented to do.

A life of significance is a life of impact. We must use egoless wisdom when deciding our vocational path. We want to dream but with our eyes open.

Lastly, I ask the key question. Do you think the dream will bring you a life of significance? Will it allow you to achieve your future vision and final legacy?

If you can fully articulate your dream and you are able to answer positively to all of these questions, the likelihood of you fulfilling your dream is strong. It really doesn't matter how outlandish the dream sounds to me or to your friends. What matters is that it is in unison with who you are and executing it is a solid possibility.

For example, a client of mine we will call Kate is a corporate executive who has risen through the ranks at a Fortune 500 company while continuously dreaming about opening a boutique clothing store. It is all she has ever wanted to do. She loves fashion, brands, textiles, textures, and putting together the perfect outfit. She said to me, "I know it sounds crazy, but I just want a little shop in my city, and I want to make it a beautiful experience. I want to help people develop their style and be able to dress effortlessly."

She went on to describe building a creative space where people could come together both in store and online. It is completely different from what she is doing now, but as we ran through the filters, we realized that it aligns with her talents, her passion, and the way she wants to show up in the world along with the impact she wants to have on people's lives.

One-on-one it corresponded perfectly with her core purpose of having a positive impact in the world by creatively working with people to care about their lives. The one thing that was holding her back was the high risk of opening and running a retail business. She had the finances, but success was not a guarantee. It came down to whether she was willing and ready to take that risk.

We started talking about the risk versus the opportunity. What is her support system like? What do her husband and kids say about that trajectory? What if it fails? What can you do to keep it from failing? Those scenarios provided her much clarity, but the power in the process was her seeing it wasn't just a pipe dream; it was something that aligned with who she is innately. Until that point, she didn't even want to say it out loud because she thought people would think she was silly. Now she proudly declares it with confidence because it is consistent with her Life Compass.

Today Kate is finalizing her business plan, working in two lanes—her current corporate role while building the new business venture—until it is time to launch. She is finally bringing color and life to the ideas she has been dreaming about for years. I can hardly wait to see her dream realized!

A Second Time up to the Plate

When I reflect on Kate's story, as well as my own, I ponder the idea of having more than one career in a lifetime. It is interesting to consider that as we age, new drives are ignited within us, which can elicit a new adventure or endeavor in our career. The idea of reinventing yourself is a foreign concept to most of our parents and definitely to our grandparents. But working in one industry or field of work for the rest of your life is not very appealing to this generation of workers. You can make a shift if it makes sense, especially if you have reached a certain level of success to provide you with a little more capacity to manage your risk. Even if that is not the case, if you're drawn to this idea of having a longer life, shifting careers and finding the right place to work is a great way to wake you back up.

Making a transition into a new industry happened rather organically for me. Once I created space to more closely examine my unique talents and passions, I was able to see that I could realize impact in a new way. Taking my decades of leadership experience and combining it with my psychology master's gave me a new approach to how I could use my unique talents.

After I left HGTV, several former coworkers and colleagues from the media industry reached out to me for advice on various situations they were wrestling through at work. I was able to connect the dots for them and systematically guide them through the next, best options. I found it enjoyable to hear their stories, and it was easy to help them process their struggles. Each time a conversation would end, I'd feel a high level of satisfaction.

It was at the urging of one of these former coworkers that I began the process of setting up my own company. My husband was doing strategic planning and finding new joy in facilitating teams to set strategic goals and execute clear vision. When we saw the synergy between our two paths, we decided to join forces and create Navigate the Journey. We have built a company that comes alongside entrepreneurial leaders and businesses to help them reach their full potential in their companies and their personal lives through strategic planning, leadership coaching, and team development.

If you had asked either of us ten years earlier if we'd ever imagine working together or owning our own business, we most certainly would have laughed. Today, we have a thriving business because we leaned into our core purposes, talents, and passions and imagined a new vision for our future. We have the opportunity for mastery and meaning every day and are enjoying the agency that is provided by owning our own company. Yes, it was a wildly risky endeavor, but it has paid off.

Shifting gears in midlife can allow you to reach creative peaks well into your older age. Daring career switches have paid off for many. Martha Stewart, a successful caterer, shifted gears into writing books and appearing on television after the age of forty-one. Vera Wang, first a successful figure skater, found after her wedding at age forty that she had a passion and drive to be a designer. Tim and Nina Zagat gave up legal careers after age forty-two to create the Zagat restaurant guides. Robin Chase was a stay-at-home mom when she and a friend came up with the idea of Zipcar. Julia Child published her first cookbook at age thirty-nine and launched a television show at age fifty-one. These are just a few examples of how the best can be yet to come!

I didn't imagine that I could have two careers in a lifetime, but they have ended up being two amazing rides. It isn't lost on me that the second career couldn't have happened until I not only reached the creative peak of midlife but gained the necessary life experience as well. I could not have written this book ten years ago, before the experience I had gained leaving my corporate job, moving across the country, raising two grown children, and growing another company to success. I had to live those experiences and gain that wisdom to write from a place of integrity and expertise. Some career changes need time before they can be successful endeavors.

I am proud of the success I have achieved but even prouder of the significance I have had on the lives of others. And who knows what the future holds. I may have another adventure up my sleeve!

Staring Fear in the Face

Charting a new course for our career exposes the place where some of our deepest vulnerabilities lie. It's important to acknowledge the very real fear that keeps us from stepping up to the plate once again. Only by looking fear in the face can we discover what's on the other side.

Many people have been taught to suppress their dreams and remain pragmatic. Other people are serial entrepreneurs and have failed at many attempted dreams in the past, sometimes at great financial costs. Some people are convinced they shouldn't make waves. They have a "good enough" life. This thinking is often fueled by the fact that they have gotten further than their parents ever did and feel guilty for wanting more.

Sometimes, regardless of our due diligence, the fear of the unknown can buckle us. A series of scary what-if questions pop into our heads, but what becomes scarier is how it paralyzes us from choosing a new beginning. What if we are so fearful about what's to come we miss creating a life we actually want?

Of all the fears my clients raise when examining the next best option for their vocational life, it is fear of not having enough money that is the most repeated. When examining your own fear of not having enough, you may find that there is another, even deeper fear at the root.

A fear of not having enough money seems rational if you are struggling to make ends meet, you have bounced a couple of checks, or your job seems unsteady. But this fear is also present with people who have had a steady paycheck for decades, have enjoyed a successful career, and seem to have a fair amount of money in the bank. Yet the fear persists. You wake up and go to the job you've come to dread, or have fallen out of love with, and you sit at your desk looking out the window fantasizing about what you'd really like to do. You have looked at the numbers and know that you have enough to get your new idea off the ground, yet you put your dream aside and dive back into the mundane. The math makes sense, but you still have that one voice pounding out the same statement in your head—*What if... what if I don't have enough?... what if I have enough to survive but not enough to thrive?*

During coaching calls with my clients, I let them ask these questions out loud enough times until they land on the real question at hand—what if *I'm* not enough? What if I can't pull it off? What if I fail?

So many deep fears are baked into these haunting questions. Are we going to be defined the rest of our lives by this next pivot? If it doesn't succeed, will we then be thought of as a failure? If our bank account drains and we can't take that next fabulous vacation, will we then be defined by lack of wealth? What if you can't withstand the pressure? What if the successful world you have so carefully crafted unravels?

During a Tribeca TV Festival in New York City in 2017, Oprah Winfrey recalled, "Everybody that I ever interviewed after every interview at some point somebody would say, 'How was that? Was that okay? How'd I do?' And that is whether it was Barack Obama or Beyoncé or the guy who murdered his kids or the guy who molested kids or somebody who had gone on and lost their family." Winfrey called this question the "common denominator" for all her guests no matter who they are, saying, "Everybody just wants to know that you heard me, you saw me, and that what I said mattered."

The questioning of our performance points to the longings within us. Those longings are what lie beneath our fears. We must understand those longings and be able to meet them with an open heart. It is then we will be able to release our fears around our performance, possibility of failure, and subsequently, not being able to provide for ourselves and our families.

Of course, I do not know what the future holds. What I can say is that if you have once been successful and you are following a vision based on your true innate gifting, talents, and passions, the likelihood of succeeding again is very high. You are a horse I am willing to bet on. Now you need to be willing to bet on yourself. What would you do if you weren't afraid? What would you choose next?

MAKE YOUR WORK MATTER

We can master our crafts and find financial freedom in our job, but if we do not consider our work meaningful, then we will miss the mark of a fulfilling vocation. After all, human beings are meaning-makers; we rely on meaning to give us hope and confidence to keep fighting the good fight.

The noted English architect Sir Christopher Wren was supervising the construction of a magnificent cathedral in London. Wren, who was unknown by most of his laborers, stopped and asked three different people who were performing the same job what they were doing. He received three different answers. The first replied, "I'm cutting this stone." The next person answered, "I am earning three shillings, six pence a day." But the third said, "I'm helping Sir Christopher Wren build this great cathedral."

Beyond a task or a way to make a living, the third laborer was able to see the meaning behind their work and the greater good they were producing. The same can be true for each of us.

Maybe the biggest lesson from *It's a Wonderful Life* comes as George Bailey processes his near-death experience. Upon seeing how life would look for his family, friends, and community without himself in it, George's perspective powerfully shifts. For the first time he clearly recognizes his unique contribution to the world around him. Clarence, the angel, sums up the epiphany when he says to George, "Each man's life touches so many other lives. When he isn't around, he leaves an awful hole, doesn't he?"

Turns out George wasn't in a dead-end job in a dead-end town, only living a modest yet significant life. Suddenly, and without any of his circumstances changing, George realizes he is actually "the richest man in town."

It's time to let go of our limited perspectives on work and give ourselves permission to make our work matter. A commitment to finding renewed motivation, real fulfillment, and the right place to work will have you well on your way to a meaningful work life you want—marked not by earnings, time, or title but by significance.

Reflections

- What do you like or dislike about your current vocational work?
- Is there opportunity to use your talents, passion, and purpose in your current role or in your current company?
- Do you feel like you are doing good work that aligns to your core values?
- Are you able to work toward mastery, with agency, and feel a connection to those around you? Do you have any dreams you long to realize?

PART THREE

WHERE AM I GOING?

The only thing worse than being blind
is having sight but no vision.

—HELEN KELLER

CHAPTER TEN

YOUR FUTURE

"All men dream but not equally.
Those who dream by night in the dusty recesses
of their minds awake to the day to find it was all vanity.
But the dreamers of the day are dangerous men,
for the many act out their dreams with
open eyes, to make it possible..."

—T.E. LAWRENCE, LAWRENCE OF ARABIA

On January 15, 2009, US Airways flight 1549 lost both its engines after being hit by a flock of geese seconds after takeoff from LaGuardia Airport. Captain Chesley Sullenberger, the plane's pilot, masterfully decided how and where to land the plane, and then safely landed it all in just over three minutes.

The plane being flown that morning was an Airbus A320 with what is called a glass cockpit. The gauges run on electronics, and if power is lost, they go dark. Within seconds of the collision, Captain Sully, as he is now known to us, turned on the auxiliary generator, keeping one very important gauge working. The gauge he needed, called a green dot gauge, determined what angle the plane needed to fly in order to go as far as possible.

Captain Sully had decided within seconds that the best option for survival of his passengers was to land in the Hudson River. But not just anywhere in the Hudson River. He wanted to land near Forty-Second Street, knowing that was the location of the ferry terminals. It was an extremely cold day in New York City, and he knew people would need to be rescued immediately from the frigid water.

While the gauge was doing the work of keeping the plane at the exact angle it needed to be, Captain Sully considered all the other action steps he needed to take. This gauge helped him get clear. It enabled him simplify and decide. It allowed him to focus on what was most important—the lives he wanted to save.

Sully recounted, "...I quickly set priorities, I *load shed*—pared down this problem to its essential elements—did the few things that had to be done, did them very well, and I was willing to *goal sacrifice*. I knew that the highest priority was to save lives, and I was more than willing to give up trying to save the airplane very early on in order to do that."[51]

Sometimes we can feel like we've been smacked by a flock of geese and the engines are down. We have lost focus and clarity. Our life is living us instead of us living it. Our lack of clarity has led to wasted moments, days, or even years of our life. We are just a passenger and no longer the pilot.

The goal of creating a strategic plan for your life is not to make things more complicated but to simplify your future by focusing and getting clear on exactly who you are and where you want to go. In a sense, you are load shedding or focusing energy on the areas of essential priority, landing you precisely in the life you want.

Just like the green dot gauge enabled Sully to gain back command of what seemed like an uncontrollable situation, your vision is the green dot gauge for your future. It is designed to help you gain back control of what seems out of control and keep you on track to go as far in your journey as possible.

THE POWER OF VISION

When I was first starting out at HGTV, the head of our division introduced our team to the idea of imagining and articulating a personal vision. Our small group met together to do some team bonding. He instructed us to write our future selves a letter, one year from the current date. We all received a stamped envelope to write our address, insert the letter, and return to him. He promised to mail it in the future.

I remember the day, one year later, when I opened the letter. I had a clear memory of writing it but only a vague recollection of its contents. I was surprised to read specific details of what I had hoped would happen that had indeed come to fruition. I had implanted so many ideas and dreams into my psyche, and several of them had become a reality. It was at that moment when I was sold on the power of creating a vivid and detailed picture of a future desired destination. The exercise showed me that writing down our hopes and dreams has real power. We can create a picture of our ideal future that is not only an inspiration but a guide we can reference regularly.

THE PERFECT ROAD TRIP

When we map out our destination on a road trip, the journey is less stressful and more enjoyable. We are able to decide exactly how we want to get there and in what amount of time, and name the stops along the way. We become excited as we plan, knowing the payoff at the end.

The same is true for your Life Vision. When you know where you are headed, you have more control of your journey along the way.

Your Vision Gets Everyone in the Car

Articulating your vision brings alignment to all areas in your life. You know who is on the journey with you, and you make sure not to leave the essentials behind. There are only so many seats in the car so you are sure not to get overcrowded, but there is room enough for the people and things that matter most.

Your Vision Makes You the Driver

A driver keeps their eyes on the road and facing front. You do not ruminate on the past or dwell in regret. You look forward with hope and excitement for what lies ahead. You are at the steering wheel and not in the back seat. You are still able to fully enjoy the journey but keep yourself on the right road, which gives you confidence and peace.

Your Vision Manages Roadblocks

Roadblocks and speed bumps are inevitable, but when you know where you are going you can avoid some and manage the others. You are better able to anticipate the ups and downs of the journey because you keep your eyes on the prize of reaching your destination. The GPS stays on so you can course correct after missed exits or wrong turns and adjust your expectations if there is traffic along the way.

THE FORMATION OF VISION

> *"Begin with the end in mind."*
>
> —STEPHEN COVEY

There is a classic saying: "If you don't know where you are going, any road will take you there." It is often used as a warning that if you don't have a set vision or destination, you may end up either nowhere in particular or someplace you do not like.

When working with companies to develop a strategic plan, we begin as early as possible in the process crafting a clear and complete picture of where the CEO and their team would like to take the business. We wisely name the destination and begin with the end in mind.

Most of our clients want to immediately jump from articulating their company's core purpose to creating strategy on how to accomplish it. I'm a type A person as well, so it's often hard for me not to jump directly into "what you should do next" mode. But when you clearly state exactly where you want to end up, you can create the right strategies to get there.

By going through the process of discovering and defining your unique talents, passions, and personal purpose, you are suddenly awakened to new inspiration and therefore new possibilities. This realization demands a new journey, a new path, and a reimagined future.

Sharpening Your Vision

To get to where you really want to go you need to name the destination. You must pause and paint a full and detailed picture of what you hope your life will look like in the future.

Our vision statement is our *where*. It is an ultimate picture, a dream, of you enjoying the fruits of living out your purpose. It is your future. It is a conscious, well-thought-out statement, informed by the points on your Life Compass: your talents, passions, values, and purpose. Your vision also takes into consideration what and who is most important to you.

A powerful first step in creating a vision statement for your future is to imagine the legacy you wish to leave behind. While vision is looking forward, legacy is looking back on your life. It is two sides of the same coin. Considering one side of that coin first helps you craft the other.

How Do You Want to Be Remembered?

In 1867, Swedish chemist Alfred Nobel awoke one morning to read his own obituary in the local paper:

> Alfred Nobel, the inventor of dynamite, who died yesterday, devised a way for more people to be killed in a war than ever before. He died a very rich man.

Actually, it was Alfred's older brother who had died; a newspaper reporter had made a mistake. But the account had a profound effect on Alfred. He decided he wanted to be known for something other than developing a means to kill people efficiently and amassing a fortune in the process. Nobel initiated the Nobel Prize—an award for scientists and writers who foster peace. "Every man ought to have the chance to correct his epitaph in midstream and write a new one," Nobel said.

Legacy is such a heavy word. We can get lost in the weightiness of it and believe it only belongs to those who have won a Nobel Prize. But legacy is simply the influence we had on the people we touched with our lives. It is the imprint we made during our days on this planet. Yes, some people's imprints may be wider than ours, but the depth is truly up to us.

In general, people want to live a long life, yet we don't like the idea of getting older. Worse yet, we don't like the idea of dying and considering those we will leave behind. But if there is one certainty in life it is that we will one day die and most likely leave behind some kind of memory of who we were and what we did while we were here.

> ***Instead of lamenting getting older, we can embrace the years ahead to solidify our legacy.***

Legacy is our gift to the people in our life. What is the gift you hope to leave behind? A simple yet profound exercise to help you clarify your lasting contribution to the world is crafting a Legacy Statement.

Close your eyes and imagine you are sitting in the back row of your own funeral. You see your coffin at the front. You are at peace. You have lived a long and happy life. The room is filled with your family and friends celebrating a life well lived. One after another, they take the stage, stand at the podium and say just one sentence about you. Each person says the same sentence, over and over again. What is that one sentence? What is the sentence that would fill you with pride and joy if you heard it repeated at your funeral? Said by your spouse, your children, your coworkers, your neighbors, and your friends. What do you ultimately want the impact of your life to be?

Forcing ourselves to think of one sentence that would span across all types of people in our lives helps us to see that we can live out our purpose in multiple ways. This exercise, if done correctly, can be a transcendent experience. It can and should invoke tears. Tears because it's hard to think of our death so clearly. Tears because we hope there would be such a great thing said about us. Tears because we realize there is much left to do and a better way to be.

This exercise digs deep into your soul. It is a glimpse into the vision you hope for in the second half of your life. The words of your Legacy Statement are a glimpse into your heart.

Kerry Egan, a Harvard Divinity School-trained hospital chaplain, writes in her book *On Living*, "If there is any great difference between the people who know they are dying and the rest of us, it's this: They know they are running out of time. They have more motivation to do the things they want to do, and to become the person they want to become... There's nothing stopping you from acting with the same urgency the dying feel."

A Vivid Vision

Our Legacy Statement is a picture of the person we hope to be, the best version of ourselves. It is an important anchor to a significant life. Our next step is to paint a vivid picture of how we imagine our entire life will look in the future.

Writing a vision statement is also a powerful journey into your imagination. It is a process of stepping into the future and articulating out loud the life you have created as if it has already happened. To many, the idea of creating a vision of the future seems elusive, but after going through the exercise of crafting a Life Compass, writing a vision statement should flow rather easily.

How deep in the future we imagine depends on where you are now and how far you are hoping to go. A first step is to state the exact age you want to live until. Of course, we have absolutely no control over the date of our death, but naming how long you want to live helps many people see that there is a lot of road left in their journey. It provides hope and focus. Resigning yourself to believing the best days are behind you or assuming you will golf your life away tends to dissipate when you realize that leaves a lot of years of golfing.

I would like to live until I am 105 years old.

I picked this age because I am dedicated to a longevity mindset and believe I can get there if I fully commit to all areas of my personal health and surround myself with my village. I desire an older age if I can live a healthy and engaged life right up to the end. I desire to live long enough to continue to enjoy my marriage, support and love my daughters fully, and to have a relationship with my grandchildren, should I become a grandmother. When I initially wrote a number in my nineties, it just didn't seem like enough time. I decided to go for it. Becoming a centurion no longer feels so out of reach!

Next, name your age twenty-five years in the future. This is a good place to imagine yourself as you design a long-term vision statement.

As I am writing this, I am fifty-one years old. I write my vision statement as if I am seventy-six years old.

A whole, purposeful, and significant Life Vision is one that has a beautiful sentence or two next to each of your Life Zones. Therefore, a vision statement is a full paragraph rather than just one sentence.

It is not a picture of a perfect person or a perfect life but a picture of someone who is grateful, fulfilled, and whole. Someone who is not riddled with regret or blocked by fear but has gratitude for experiencing a life well-lived.

It is helpful to vividly picture the big and small details of your life. What does your home look like? Envision your family, including your future grandchildren around you. See your spouse or life partner next to you. Imagine the faces of the people you have influenced and touched over the years. See your neighborhood. Picture the places you hope to go. Do you want to climb a mountain or go to an exotic land? Picture yourself there. Imagine the taste of the food and the smell in the air. Bring your future to life in your mind. The power of your mind is real.

A vision statement does not include any strategy. It does not tell us how to get there; it merely illustrates your life a few decades down the road. It is a picture of a real person who has lived a real life. A good vision statement is authentic to you. It should be meaningful not only to you but to others, should they read it.

Your vision should be somewhat grand in nature. It should have what I like to call a faith gap, meaning it will take a great deal of faith to get there. You know you most likely won't be able to achieve it alone. You also understand that you'll need to lean more into the optimistic corners of your heart, which should be easier now that you have a truer sense of your gifts and talents.

Lastly, your vision statement should move you. It should tug hard at your heart and resonate deeply in your soul. You should read it and think, *That is beautiful. That is amazing. Oh, how I long to make that a reality.*

REALIZING YOUR VISION

> *"Vision without execution is hallucination."*
>
> —THOMAS EDISON

In Stephen Covey's *The 7 Habits of Highly Effective People*, he writes about how all things are created twice. There is first a mental creation followed by a physical or second creation. He uses the creation of a home as an example.

> You create it in every detail before you ever hammer the first nail into place. You try to get a clear sense of what kind of house you want... You work with ideas. You work with your mind until you get a clear image of what you want to build. You have to make sure that the blueprint, the first creation, is really what you want, that you've thought everything through. Then you put it into bricks and mortar.

At this point in the book, you have developed your first creation. You have examined your past and articulated your unique design, discovering more deeply the internal fingerprint of your life. You have dreamt of a lofty and vivid vision of the future.

Now it is time for the second creation. It is time to move the bricks and mortar into place. One brick at a time, you will execute your first creation, putting action to those dreams.

Prioritizing Your Vision

There is a great deal of tension between strategy and execution. Too many business executives spend a large amount of time and energy developing a solid strategy only to fall short upon execution. Leaders don't consciously decide to do this. Their well-crafted vision just evaporates as the daily grind gets in the way.

The same can be true when executing the strategic map you have created for the life you want. You put the hard work into understanding your past and present and setting a clear destination for your future. You even develop key initiatives and action steps, but you put it on the shelf and only half implement it into your life.

Why does this happen?

Chris McChesney, in his book *The 4 Disciplines of Execution*, says that all humans have one trait in common that keeps us from executing our plans: our tendency to move toward urgency. The needs of the day always win. We often must talk ourselves into doing something that isn't urgent, despite its importance.

McChesney calls it "the whirlwind." He uses it in reference to the business day, but it's easily applicable to your life as a whole. We often get caught up in the whirlwind of all the pressures, demands, urgent needs, and must-dos of each day. The whirlwind is good at keeping us alive but is also good at rejecting things. It distracts and derails us. Before we know it, our strategic plans, in all their beauty, become dusty and lose their shine. We have conversations that begin with "remember when I was going to..." Our lives run us rather than us running our lives. Eventually, our vision is suffocated by our daily routines.

The whirlwind is not going to go away. The key is learning how to navigate it.

Filling Your Bucket

Navigating the whirlwind of our lives starts with a commitment to actionable and measurable goals. A helpful framework for setting those goals is called Big Rocks. The origin of the concept of Big Rocks is unknown, but it was popularized by Covey in his book *The 7 Habits of Highly Effective People.*

Covey imagines how best to fill a bucket with rocks, pebbles, and sand. The bucket is your life. Rocks represent the highest, non-negotiable goals that will get you to your ideal vision. Pebbles represent the things we love or need to do but aren't crucial. The sand represents the mundane day-to-day tasks.

The concept is not about filling your bucket but what you can fit into your bucket depending on what you put in first. If you first put in the big rocks (i.e., do the big things), there is still space for the pebbles and the sand, but if you fill the bucket in reverse, starting with the sand, you'll never be able to add the big rocks. You prohibit yourself from accomplishing your most important goals because your bucket is filled with minutia.

Mindless busyness is taking up too much space in our buckets. Busyness does not equal productivity. Busyness does not make you seem more important or in demand.

Busyness should not be an identity.

The only thing you get out of being too busy is stress.

To make space for a life of significance you need balance, intention, and focus. With your articulated purpose, vision, talents, and values, you should have more clarity than you have had in years. This clarity will allow you to rid yourself of all the unnecessary busyness in your life so you can focus on the key priorities.

When strategically planning for our life, we call these key priorities Life Rocks.

Setting Life Rocks

Your long-term vision is only as strong as the short-term priorities that hold it up. To turn your dream into a reality, it's time to name and claim these non-negotiable goals called Life Rocks.

Dr. Gail Matthews, psychologist and researcher, states that you are 42 percent more likely to achieve a goal by simply writing it down. The reason for such an increase? The simple act of writing it down crystallizes what you need to accomplish. It turns out this clarity is also very motivating.

Your Life Rocks don't address everything in your life—just your current key priorities that will positively affect your ultimate vision.

Identify one Life Rock for each Life Zone—personal health, family, friends, community, and work. Write a clear and measurable objective for each Life Rock and consider at least three strategic action steps to execute over the coming ninety days. This process will get you on a quarterly rhythm of focus. Once you commit and develop your rhythm, goal setting will become a habit. That habit will ensure vision success!

Ultimately, goal setting is critical in taking the long view and achieving your new definition of success—your vision. Your Life Rocks will serve as a decision-making filter, ensuring that you make wise decisions moving forward. They will give you balance and perspective as you navigate your life.

These goals will give you power through increased clarity. That power leads to less anxiety and stress. Putting the goals into a ninety-day window begins to give you direction and control over what lies ahead. It makes the perspective that you have gathered throughout your life map creation process actionable, accurate, and achievable.

Shooting for the Moon

In the bestselling business book *Built to Last*, author Jim Collins talks about the importance of companies outlining a Big Hairy Audacious Goal (BHAG). A BHAG is a long-term goal that is guided by a company's core purpose and core values. It is so audacious, out of the box, and hairy that you feel like you may never achieve it. We have found the creation of BHAGs for companies to be an exciting and energizing tool. It keeps them from thinking too small and stretches their visionary skills. It forces you to think big. As we know from history, those who have big dreams can accomplish extraordinary things.

In 1961, President John F. Kennedy famously announced that he wanted to put a man on the moon. At the time, his goal had less than a 50 percent chance of being achieved given current technology. But this didn't keep it from happening. Naming and claiming this big, hairy, and audacious goal galvanized NASA and the entire United States during an uncertain Cold War era. It became an inspiring hope for the country.

After the success of going to the moon, the term *moonshot* entered the lexicon. Its meaning is listed as "a difficult task, the outcome of which is expected to have great significance." I believe everyone should always have one Moonshot Goal they are working on in their life. It's big yet galvanizing because it is truly connected to your purpose and values, and therefore not impossible. It is one idea that is part of your overall vision but stands out for its audacity. Once you achieve your Moonshot Goal, you create another one that aligns with your long-term vision and even helps propel it.

Your Moonshot Goal is the top of your Mount Everest rather than the boundary of your backyard. It is unique to you. What feels big to you may not feel like a stretch for someone else, and that's okay. A Moonshot Goal is typically a dream, creation, or secret longing. It has been tucked away in the back of your mind or been verbalized constantly but hasn't yet been fully brought to life.

Moonshot Goals can make us better because they often stimulate growth and demand progress. They energize us and make us feel alive.

Making a bold move and taking a risk is a big part of realizing the grandest vision for yourself. Only fear will keep you from making it a reality. Don't give your fear power. Dream of that Moonshot Goal and continually move toward it.

My Moonshot Goal was writing a book. Many things held me back from writing this book earlier. Age, experience, and time to name a few. But the number one reason was fear. Fear has held me back from writing a book for nearly ten years. Fear that I am not smart enough or gifted enough as a writer. Fear of what other people will think and say; fear that it will not be deemed a success by whomever does the deeming.

It wasn't until I named my fear and let it go that I was able to take the leap. It didn't make it less scary, but it did give me the courage, knees knocking, to pull the trigger and say out loud and to my friends and family, "I am doing it."

Writing a book is big and on most days it felt rather hairy, but I took the leap. While I am not certain it will be a raving success, one thing I can be confident of is that not writing it won't be a regret I harbor when I am much older. Turns out summoning the courage to write this book was a practice in applying significance over success!

You are reading this book which means I achieved my Moonshot Goal. Therefore, it is time for me to create a new one. I have decided that I would like to use my platform as a way to influence and help others. My new Moonshot Goal is to help one million people live to their full potential. It will take time and effort, but if I strategically lean into using my book, podcast, and speaking engagements, I believe I can get there. It is a new, exciting, and scary enough prospect to keep me moving and growing!

Your Moonshot Goal should be a goal that if achieved will positively impact several areas of your life. For instance, my husband has a Moonshot Goal of being able to cycle one hundred miles a week at age seventy-five. He realizes that it will take time and effort to reach this goal, but he also knows that it will be well worth it. The positive ripple effects of achieving this goal are part of his motivation. He knows he'll need to be in optimal health, which will increase his longevity. Being healthy into his older years also means he will have the energy to be a good husband, father, and potential grandfather. He also knows this goal will help keep his mind sharp and focused.

Life's greatest adventures take courage. New beginnings take courage, because naysayers exist. They always will. They cause you to suppress some part of you. They make you believe that putting yourself out there or drawing attention to yourself is arrogant. They make you feel like you aren't smart enough or allowed to use your platform. They make you doubt yourself. They make you pull back.

But if your intentions are rooted in purpose and your motivations are good, then pulling back is robbing yourself and others from your best contribution. Pulling yourself out of the fabric makes that fabric weaker.

Your biggest achievement could be fulfilling your own dream, the one *you* want, not the one someone else dreamt for you. Pursuing someone else's vision is soul sucking and will leave you depleted, empty, and even angry.

Sometimes you are waiting for a door to open, not realizing you already hold the key. You need to find the courage to unlock the door, open it, and step through. Time is fleeting. Don't miss your opportunity. The door may not remain. Stop staring at it. Grab the handle.

Your story is yours. You own your future chapters—no one else. Life will add its own color to these chapters, but you are the author.

You write the story. Your talents, passions, purpose, and values are the tools of your craft. Your story comes more fully into being by setting the goals needed to realize your vision. This is how you become the protagonist. Envision it. Own it. Begin again. For yourself. Don't let someone else or something else rob you of being the hero of your story.

THE PROTECTION OF VISION

> *"Discipline is the bridge between goals and accomplishment."*
>
> —JIM ROHN

You've just spent a lot of valuable time setting strategic goals to ensure you reach your life's vision. While it took work to get there, in some sense, setting the goals is the easy part. You may feel very motivated right now and ready to dig into a brighter future. But if you do not have the discipline to stick to your plan and execute your goals, it will be difficult, if not impossible, to realize your full, articulated vision.

> ***Discipline will take you places motivation cannot.***

Motivation is an amazing tool and can take you far. It can propel you to buy the Peloton, purchase the cycling shoes, and even put on the new workout outfit. But motivation alone will not get you on the bike without fail each and every week.

Motivation dries up easily because it is based on feelings. Discipline is based on action. Motivation may get the wheels turning, but discipline takes you to the finish line.

Living a life of significance takes self-control, intention, and most of all, discipline. Discipline keeps temptation at bay. It is what turns goals into habits and habits into routine. We need to create routine to resist instant gratification and our innate desire to find comfort first.

For some people, discipline is easy. They are driven by process and detail. They are naturally gifted at taking a project from start to finish without much derailment. It seems almost intuitive for them.

For others, the idea of the end goal is ten times more exciting than the execution to get there. They become easily distracted, procrastinating often. These are the people for whom execution tools are essential.

The life map you have created is for the rest of your life. It is exciting and filled with hopes and dreams. But how do you live all of this out? How are you going to realize this best version of yourself?

I am ending this book by listing a variety of tools that will help you live the life you want. You know yourself best. You know which ones will work for you. Regardless of what you choose, I encourage you to commit. Commit to your life map. Commit to your vision. Execute the goals you have outlined in order to get there.

Measuring Your Results

> *"However beautiful the strategy, you should occasionally look at the results."*
>
> **—WINSTON CHURCHILL**

When my daughter was in the fourth grade, she joined the basketball team. There is nothing cuter than watching eight-year-olds from a Montessori school play basketball for the first time. Once we reminded them that we don't share the ball or take turns with the other team, things started to take shape. As they understood how the game worked and how they could win, they became more competitive.

One game in particular became rather exciting as the score was very close. Suddenly the scoreboard broke. After a few minutes and a couple more baskets, the kids lost track of what the score was. They were confused and disoriented. It hadn't dawned on me how important it is to a team to know how they are doing in order to win. They needed their scoreboard to properly play the game!

The same holds true for us at work and in life. We are more focused and clearer on our end goal if we know how we are measuring up. Measuring our game reminds us of our progress. It gives us the clarity and energy to keep moving forward. Keeping a scorecard or a monthly tracker and looking at it regularly is an important tool to keep you on track.

Monthly Review

In the weeks following the emergency landing of Flight 1549, a US Airways flight attendant noticed that all her passengers took out their safety cards and followed along during her safety demonstrations. She hadn't received that kind of attention from passengers in her thirty years of flying. It took a rather scary event for people to remember that the safety card in the seatback pocket existed and has beneficial information to ensure survival.

For our life journey we have created a monthly review tool not just to ensure survival but so you thrive with your life map. You can use our Strategic Life Map Tracker to monitor and maintain your progress. Download a free **Strategic Life Map Tracker** from tracischubertbarrett.com and fill in all the key elements.

Each month, have a time locked in on your calendar to check in with your Strategic Life Map Tracker. During your check-in, reread all the elements of your life map. Read your core purpose statement, each of your core values, each of your unique talents, your passion, and finally your complete vision statement.

You will then review your Life Rocks and your Moonshot Goal. Assess where you are today, how much progress you have made, and how much is left to complete your goal. You will also take time to reflect on each of your Life Zones. Be sure to take a pulse on your level of connection and commitment to yourself and those around you.

Win Your Week

On a weekly basis, write a very short list of the things you must complete for the coming week to make it feel like a win. Do the list, win the week!

Make sure the list aligns with your overall goals and vision. Don't mistake whirlwind activities with actions taken toward your vision. This isn't a to-do list. It is a list that aligns to your Tracker. Don't write "take Sally to the dentist" or "make a hair appointment." Instead write a list of things that will help you move the needle on your Life Rocks.

- Make four follow-up calls on new job opportunities.
- Walk the dog three times for physical health.
- Write one blog post.
- Book a date night with my spouse.

Creating these monthly and weekly types of commitments will develop habits that will change your behavior for the long term. Your change in behavior will guarantee success. It is the small steps and the little wins that keep us going and create forever habits.

Stay committed. Don't give up. Don't let your plan gather dust and be forgotten. Having measurable goals is essential to reaching your dream vision.

Accountability Partners

Captain Sully didn't land the plane on the Hudson all by himself. He had a talented copilot named Jeff Skiles by his side. I imagine the likelihood of a successful landing would have been compromised if Sully had been alone.

The same is true for executing your life map. Don't go it alone. Ask those wise and trusted friends, family members, mentors, and colleagues for feedback. You must insist on honesty with the answers. You must continue to see your true self—the good and the bad—let go of the false stories you tell yourself, and commit to growth all while being free in who you are.

> *"Our chief want in life is somebody who will make us do what we can."*
>
> **—RALPH WALDO EMERSON**

You are more likely to have a successful journey if you have trusted people in your life holding you accountable. Accountability can scare some people because they feel a loss of control when they let others in. Other people just don't want to hear they are wrong or off track. Those who welcome loving support and are open to challenge are the people who are most likely to realize their vision.

Bringing people into your newly found world of purpose and direction is also rewarding. Sharing all the hard work you put into strategically planning your life can be a satisfying experience.

If you have a spouse or life partner, sharing your life map can be a very beautiful experience. When couples commit to this process simultaneously, you see a whole new connection in the relationship.

Suddenly you are sharing a combined vision. You can fully support each other in your outlined goals and action steps.

My husband and I have carved out a day each year between Christmas and New Year's to refresh our goals and remind each other of each of the elements that comprise our life maps. We analyze and then make tweaks where necessary and discuss what our hopes are for the coming year. We have a vested interest in seeing each other's vision come to fruition. A happy, healthy partner is a wonderful gift. We want to give that gift to each other.

Creating a specific support system that matches your needs may consist of finding a mentor, coach, or therapist. It may include reaching out to an old colleague or friend. A support system can be essential in getting the help you may need not only to execute upon your life map but to support you as you practice the new habits and ways of thinking.

Celebrate Your Accomplishments

Sometimes we slip right past our achievements and start immediately planning our next goal. This can derail us and lead to burnout. The easiest way to avoid burnout is to celebrate your wins, even the small ones. Each time you complete a rock, celebrate. Come up with a ritual or list of rewards. Maybe it is a massage or a trip away. Maybe you buy a new book or a new outfit. Maybe you call a friend to catch up and grab lunch. Perhaps you just allow yourself a couple of hours on the back porch to relax and unwind. The goal is to create a moment or a space where you are actually patting yourself on the back.

Relish the sweet feeling of success. You are officially living a life of significance!

Annual Renewal

I do have one non-negotiable when it comes to execution tools for your life map. No matter how innately disciplined you are or are not, you must revisit and revise your life map annually. As I mentioned I do with my husband, once a year, ideally at the same time every year, open all of your life map elements: Life Compass, Life Vision, Legacy Statement, current Life Rocks, and your one Moonshot Goal. Review past patterns and rate how you are doing with healthy mindsets. Examine your personal health and think deeply about your current village. Rate each of these life map elements. How are you doing? What needs to be revised? Once you have updated your life map, make a renewed commitment to living it out over the coming year.

Taking time out each year for renewal not only keeps your life map top of mind but ensures that you remain on track to your envisioned future. It is your best tool for making sure you are living the significant life you want.

ENJOY THE RIDE

My hope is that the process of creating a life you want brings clarity, commitment, and excitement. Whatever your life has been up to this point, it does not dictate the future. Your past success has been great, but it is not the end. Not even close.

Today's problems exist, as will tomorrow's, but you have a new outlook and set of tools to conquer them and move forward. Hold on tightly to your Life Compass so you do not lose your way. Your vision statement is your final destination. Move toward that destination with hope and determination. Remember that it is your journey that is most important. Savor it. Your unwavering commitment will bring you the life of significance you have always desired.

Reflections

- Take time to complete the Legacy Statement Exercise.
- Sketch out your Life Vision Statement.
- Reflecting upon each of these statements, what are the steps you need to take in order to get there?
- Create at least one Life Rock for each Life Zone and outline action steps for each.

CONCLUSION

At the end of my career at HGTV, I was thrown one hell of a going-away party. My bosses rented out a restaurant and we ate, drank, and partied until the late hours. It was the cherry on top of an amazing adventure filled with success and growth.

What I realized in the middle of my going-away party was that the success I had experienced wasn't the end of my story. There were more chapters to write.

I was overwhelmed by how many of my colleagues and clients came out to wish me well. While I was looking for a nice ending to this chapter, I had no idea their words of affirmation would fill me with a new sense of confidence for the many chapters that lie ahead.

They weren't celebrating me for the amount of money that I brought into HGTV or even for helping bring the network to life. Instead, I was celebrated for how I led, how I cared, and what I gave of myself. Hearing it made me wish I had done even more of that.

What if I had gone through a strategic planning process for my life prior to leaving the network? What if I had been able to gain more clarity on who I was and why I was there? Maybe I would have stayed, doubled down, and given more to the company. Maybe I would have exited the building even sooner to begin my new career and next chapter in life. We will never know.

While the speeches were commencing, it hit me that I should say something other than just thank you. I hadn't prepared anything in advance, but one image popped clearly into my mind.

The Wizard of Oz.

Growing up it was always a favorite movie of mine. Every year, it would come on network television, and we would never miss it. We'd hunker down on the couch with a big bowl of popcorn, hide under the blanket when the flying monkeys appeared, and smile from ear to ear when Dorothy returned home. I told my colleagues that I felt like HGTV had been this amazing dream that took me on a long, yellow brick road filled with adventures and intrigue, but now it was time to click my red ruby slippers and return home.

The great philosopher Joseph Campbell famously called *The Wizard of Oz* "a hero's journey." Dorothy was the hero. Campbell said that the yellow brick road represented the path toward Dorothy's true self. Along her journey, she encountered the disempowered parts of herself: the scarecrow's wish for a brain, the tin man's desire for a heart, the cowardly lion's longing for courage.

Like so many of us, Dorothy believed she needed something outside herself to find her way. In her case, she required the great and powerful Oz to bestow the virtues each of her friends desired and then bring her home. We all know how it turns out; the great Oz is not so great and does not have the power to grant their wishes.

But, alas, Glinda the Good Witch arrives and says the words that unlock the meaning of the entire journey.

"You don't need to be helped any longer. You've always had the power."

Upon which the scarecrow asks Glinda, "Then why didn't you tell her before?"

Glinda replies, "Because she wouldn't have believed me. She had to learn it for herself."

She had to learn it for herself. I had to learn it for myself. We all have to learn it for ourselves.

No matter how far away from yourself you may have strayed on your journey to and from success, there is a path back to you—a path of significance.

You can take a pause and rediscover exactly who you are and how to fulfill your purpose in this lifetime. Your ruby slippers are ready to carry you home. You don't have far to go at all.

As Dorothy says right before she clicks her heels, "If I ever go looking for my heart's desire again, I won't look any further than my own backyard because if it isn't there, I never really lost it to begin with."

It is time to reclaim you and chart a new course to the life you want. The answers lie within you. In your own backyard.

ABOUT THE AUTHOR

TRACI SCHUBERT BARRETT is an entrepreneur, business owner, leadership expert, speaker, and executive coach. She is also a busy mom, wife, daughter, sister, and friend! She was part of a small team that launched the national cable television network HGTV: Home & Garden Television in 1994 and spent nearly twenty years helping to lead the network to success running their Chicago and Dallas offices. Traci decided to step away from the media world and merge her decades of experience leading, strategizing, managing, and mentoring to start Navigate the Journey, a business consulting firm that helps organizations and leaders maximize their potential.

Traci holds a B.A. in telecommunications & marketing from Indiana University. She also holds her M.A. in professional psychology from the Illinois School of Psychology. After living in the city of Chicago for twenty-five years, Traci, her husband, and their two daughters recently relocated to Nashville, Tennessee.

Connect with Traci on Instagram @tracisbarrett. Be sure to explore Traci's additional resources for unlocking a significant life at www.tracischubertbarrett.com.

ACKNOWLEDGMENTS

Writing this book was a much harder endeavor than I had ever imagined. It lived ten years in my head and took a year and a half of sitting endless hours in front of my computer writing, rewriting, editing, and finally sharing with the world. While this sounds like a lonely endeavor, it would not have happened without the love, support, and wisdom of many wonderful people.

First to my amazing husband, Tom. After so many years of obsessively collecting information and talking about this book, he said enough is enough and told me to go for it. Without his encouragement, love, and insanely intelligent insight, this book would not exist. You are my hero and champion. I love you.

To my beautiful daughters, Bronagh and Ashling. The thought of handing a hard copy of this book to each of you is what spurred me on! Thank you for cheering for me. Your belief in me kept me going on the days I wanted to give up. I hope this book inspires you and the generations of our family to come. I love you both immensely.

I want to thank my sisters, Connie and Renee; brother-in-law, Rob; and mother, Marie, for always believing in me, pushing me to write, and unconditionally loving me. For my sweet and supportive family in Ireland, especially Mary, Siobhan, and Philip. Thank you for your excitement and pride. It fueled me.

So many people helped in the process of bringing this book to life!

I must thank my partner in crime and editing guru, Jill McClain. You helped me organize my thoughts, pushed me to be more vulnerable and tell my personal stories, and made beautiful suggestions and edits. You are incredibly gifted, and I could not have done it without you.

Thank you to my fabulous publishing team! Thanks to my publishing managers, Katie and Jordan; you were both so organized, helpful, and supportive. To my writing coach, Karen—I'd still be sitting in my office writing had you not kept me on track, helped me organize my thoughts, and given me the push to put this all on paper! Thanks for all your keen advice and for helping me believe in my ability.

My sweet and generous friends who agreed to be beta readers—Burton, John, Jacki, and Connie. I can't thank you enough for your feedback! You gave me the confidence to release this to the world!

Thank you to my past HGTV colleagues and my current clients, many whom I call dear friends, for inspiring several of the thoughts in this book and for pushing me to share my wisdom. Thanks to those who helped verify my memories, agreed to write endorsements, and helped promote this book. I'd also like to thank the experts willing to meet with me to share their insights with me: Todd Henry, Dr. Bijoy John, and Susan Mettes.

I have an immense village of friends who unconditionally supported and loved on me during the writing of this book. I want to name you all but the fear of accidentally leaving a name off leaves me only to say you know who you are, and I am forever grateful.

Lastly, to the two men who always saw more in me than I did for myself, my father, Hugh, and my Uncle Joe, who I know are both smiling down from heaven at this accomplishment.

ENDNOTES

Introduction

[1] Rachel Wheeler, *We'll Live to 100—How Can We Afford It?* (Geneva: World Economic Forum, 2017), https://www3.weforum.org/docs/WEF_White_Paper_We_Will_Live_to_100.pdf.

Chapter One

[2] Jacqui Frank and Julie Bort, "Billionaire Minecraft Founder Markus Persson Proves Money Doesn't Buy Happiness," Business Insider, October 6, 2010, https://www.businessinsider.com/man-who-sold-minecraft-to-microsoft-markus-persson-success-2015-10.

[3] Andrew Delbanco, *The Real American Dream: A Meditation on Hope* (Cambridge: Harvard University Press, 2000).

[4] A. H. Maslow, "A Theory of Human Motivation," Psychological Review 50, no. 4 (1943): 430–37, https://doi.org/10.1037/h0054346.

[5] Pew Charitable Trusts, When Do Americans Plan to Retire? (Philadelphia: Pew Charitable Trusts, 2018), https://www.pewtrusts.org/-/media/assets/2018/11/whendoamericansplantoretire_final.pdf.

Chapter Two

[6] Lynn Hirschberg, "The Misfit," *Vogue*, April 1991, https://archive.vanityfair.com/article/share/bd86a835-b84c-47a7-bbec-60b9af6ea282.

[7] Stephen Covey, *The 7 Habits of Highly Effective People* (New York: Simon & Schuster, 1989).

[8] Jacinda Santora, "Key Influencer Marketing Statistics You Need to Know," Influencer Marketing Hub, last modified July 27, 2022, https://influencermarketinghub.com/influencer-marketing-statistics/.

[9] David Brooks, *The Second Mountain: The Quest for a Moral Life* (New York: Random House, 2020).

[10] Simon Sinek, *Start with Why: How Great Leaders Inspire Everyone to Take Action* (New York: Portfolio, 2009).

[11] Elizabeth Gilbert, "Your Elusive Creative Genius," February 9, 2009, TED video, 19:14, https://www.ted.com/talks/elizabeth_gilbert_your_elusive_creative_genius.

Chapter Three

[12] Dan McAdams, Ruthellen Josselson, and Amia Lieblich, *Turns in the Road: Narrative Studies of Lives in Transition* (Washington: American Psychological Association, 2001).

[13] Brené Brown, *Dare to Lead: Brave Work. Tough Conversations. Whole Hearts* (New York: Random House, 2018).

[14] V. I. Maiorov, "The Functions of Dopamine in Operant Conditioned Reflexes," *Neuroscience and Behavioral Physiology* 49 (2019): 887–93, https://doi.org/10.1007/s11055-019-00815-y.

[15] Christy Bartlett, James-Henry Holland, and Charly Iten, *Flickwerk: The Aesthetics of Mended Japanese Ceramics* (Munster: Museum für Lackkunst, 2008).

Chapter Four

[16] Christopher Bergland, "Why Do Abused Children Often Grow Up to Be Abusive Parents?" Psychology Today, May 1, 2021, https://www.psychologytoday.com/us/blog/the-athletes-way/202105/why-do-abused-children-often-grow-be-abusive-parents.

[17] Mark Manson, The Subtle Art of Not Giving a F*ck: A Counterintuitive Approach to Living a Good Life (New York: HarperCollins, 2016).

Chapter Five

[18] Caroline Leaf, Switch On Your Brain: The Key to Peak Happiness, Thinking, and Health (Grand Rapids, MI: Baker Books, 2013).

[19] "Is There a Limit to the Human Lifespan?" Wall Street Journal, June 24, 2018, https://www.wsj.com/articles/is-there-a-limit-to-the-human-lifespan-1529892420 ?mod=article_inline.

[20] Daniel J. DeNoon, "Early Retirement, Early Death?" Compass, October 20, 2005, https://www.webmd.com/healthy-aging/news/20051020/early-retirement-early -death.

[21] J. R. R. Tolkien, The Fellowship of the Ring (London: George Allen & Unwin, 1954).

[22] Adam Grant, Think Again: The Power of Knowing What You Don't Know (New York: Penguin Group, 2021).

[23] Glennon Doyle, Untamed (New York: Dial Press, 2020).

[24] David Foster Wallace, "Commencement Address," transcript of speech delivered at Kenyon College, Gambier, Ohio, May 21, 2005, https://people.math.harvard. edu/~ctm/links/culture/dfw_kenyon_commencement.html#:~:text=The%20really %20important%20kind%20of,and%20understanding%20how%20to%20think.

[25] Eddie Jaku, The Happiest Man on Earth: The Beautiful Life of an Auschwitz Survivor (London: Macmillan, 2021).

[26] James Clear, Atomic Habits: An Easy and Proven Way to Build Good Habits and Break Bad Ones (New York: Avery, 2021).

Chapter Six

[27] "Gallup's Employee Engagement Survey: Ask the Right Questions with the Q12 Survey," Gallup, accessed 2014, https://www.gallup.com/workplace/356063 /gallup-q12-employee-engagement-survey.aspx.

[28] "Clifton Strengths," Gallup, accessed 2014, https://www.gallup.com /cliftonstrengths/en/252137/home.aspx.

[29] "The Assessment," Motivation Code, accessed 2014, https://motivationcode.com /motivation-assessment/.

Chapter Seven

[30] "Prevalence of Both Diagnosed and Undiagnosed Diabetes," Centers for Disease Control and Prevention, last modified December 29, 2021, https://www.cdc.gov /diabetes/data/statistics-report/diagnosed-undiagnosed-diabetes.html.

[31] Richard F. Hamilton, "Work and Leisure: On the Reporting of Poll Results," *The Public Opinion Quarterly* 55, no. 3 (Autumn 1991): 347–56, https://doi.org/10.1086/269266.

[32] "Exercise: 15 Minutes a Day Ups Lifespan by 3 Years," Harvard Medical School, December 1, 2013, https://www.health.harvard.edu/heart-health/exercise-15-minutes-a-day-ups-lifespan-by-3-years#:~:text=Invest%20in%20a%20little%20exercise,minute%20of%20activity%20you%20add.

[33] Anne Ornish and Dean Ornish, Undo It! How Simple Lifestyle Changes Can Reverse Most Chronic Diseases (New York: Random House, 2021), 102.

[34] Eric Suni, "How Sleep Affects Immunity," Sleep Foundation, April 22, 2022, https://www.sleepfoundation.org/physical-health/how-sleep-affects-immunity.

[35] Christer Hublin et al., "Sleep and Mortality: A Population-Based 22-Year Follow-Up Study," Sleep 30, no. 10 (October 2007): 1245–53, https://doi.org/10.1093/sleep/30.10.1245.

[36] Racheal Rettner, "Just 20 Minutes of Walking May Reduce Inflammation in Your Body," Live Science, January 13, 2017, https://www.livescience.com/57498-exercise-reduces-inflammation.html.

[37] "Anxiety Disorders: Facts & Statistics," Anxiety and Depression Association of America, last modified June 27, 2022, https://adaa.org/understanding-anxiety/facts-statistics#:~:text=Anxiety%20disorders%20are%20the%20most,of%20those%20suffering%20receive%20treatment.

[38] Jennifer Liu, "US Workers Are among the Most Stressed in the World, New Gallup Report Finds," CNBC, June 15, 2021, https://www.cnbc.com/2021/06/15/gallup-us-workers-are-among-the-most-stressed-in-the-world.html.

[39] Jue Lin and Elissa Epel, "Stress and Telomere Shortening: Insights from Cellular Mechanisms," Ageing Research Reviews 73 (January 2022): 101507, https://doi.org/10.1016/j.arr.2021.101507.

[40] Eckhart Tolle, The Power of Now: A Guide to Spiritual Enlightenment (Novato, CA: New World Library, 2004).

[41] Daniel Amen, Change Your Brain, Change Your Life: The Breakthrough Program for Conquering Anxiety, Depression, Obsessiveness, Anger, and Impulsiveness (New York: Harmony, 2015).

[42] Christianna Reedy, "Our Brains May Be 100 Times More Powerful than We Thought," Futurism, March 24, 2017, https://futurism.com/our-brains-may-be-100-times-more-powerful-than-we-thought.

[43] Dr. Caroline Leaf, "How Trauma Impacts Memory," Dr. Leaf's Blog, October 3, 2021, https://drleaf.com/blogs/news/memory.

[44] Patricia Cohen, "A Sharper Mind, Middle Age and Beyond," New York Times, January 19, 2012, https://www.nytimes.com/2012/01/22/education/edlife/a-sharper-mind-middle-age-and-beyond.html.

[45] Elizabeth Scott, "How Stress Works with and against Your Memory," Very Well Mind, October 7, 2021, https://www.verywellmind.com/stress-and-your-memory-4158323.

Chapter Eight

[46] Proverbs 27:17, NIV.

[47] Matthew 22:37-39 ESV.

Chapter Nine

[48] David Zax, "Want to Be Happier at Work? Learn How from These 'Job Crafters,'" *Fast Company*, June 3, 2013, https://www.fastcompany.com/3011081/want-to-be-happier-at-work-learn-how-from-these-job-crafters.

[49] Jackie Wiles, "Employees Seek Personal Value and Purpose at Work. Be Prepared to Deliver," Gartner, January 13, 2022, https://www.gartner.com/en/articles/employees-seek-personal-value-and-purpose-at-work-be-prepared-to-deliver.

[50] Jim Collins, *Good to Great: Why Some Companies Make the Leap... and Others Don't* (New York: Harper Business, 2001).

Chapter Ten

[51] Carl Von Wodtke, "Sully Speaks Out," HistoryNet, September 7, 2016, https://www.historynet.com/sully-speaks-out/.